THE CHAMPION LEADER

HARNESSING THE POWER *of* EMOTIONAL INTELLIGENCE *to* BUILD HIGH-PERFORMING TEAMS

THE CHAMPION LEADER

CHRISTOPHER D. CONNORS

WILEY

Published by John Wiley & Sons, Inc., Hoboken, New Jersey.
Published simultaneously in Canada.

For general information on our other products and services or for technical support, please contact our Customer Care Department within the United States at (800) 762-2974, outside the United States at (317) 572-3993 or fax (317) 572-4002.

Wiley publishes in a variety of print and electronic formats and by print-on-demand. Some material included with standard print versions of this book may not be included in e-books or in print-on-demand. If this book refers to media such as a CD or DVD that is not included in the version you purchased, you may download this material at http://booksupport.wiley.com. For more information about Wiley products, visit www.wiley.com.

Library of Congress Cataloging-in-Publication Data is Available:

ISBN 9781394211333 (Paperback)
ISBN 9781394211357 (ePDF)
ISBN 9781394211340 (ePub)

Cover design: Paul McCarthy

SKY10070501_032724

To my dad, William O'Neil Connors: Thank you for being the best father—the ultimate champion of Bill, Kevin, and me. I love you always. Your remarkable legacy will live on forever in our hearts and memories. You're always with us in spirit.

Contents

The Champion Leader

The champion leader is willing to commit to a lifelong leadership education that begins with self-awareness.

The champion leader has the courage to go all-in and invest in the lives of their employees.

The champion leader focuses on both hygiene and motivating factors for every team member, and ensures these needs and wants are consistently being met.

The champion leader provides opportunities for growth and knows when to support, comfort, and challenge their employees to bring out their best.

The champion leader is accessible, real, and knows the best leadership is by example.

The champion leader is someone who leads from the heart with time-tested values such as integrity, honesty, love, belief, confidence, and respect.

The champion leader is driven, organized, inspirational, and committed to positively influencing others to achieve results and scale their impact.

The champion leader is an excellent communicator who celebrates the team's wins.

We can all play the role of *champion* for the people we lead.

We can all be a champion leader.

People Come First

I was speaking with a retired US Marine Corps colonel a few years ago about his experience serving in the military and all that he'd learned along the way. This man proudly served his country in Iraq and Afghanistan and, by all accounts, is a true American hero. He saw a lot of action during his combat tours. Now, as a civilian, he found himself pondering what leadership meant to him: how it helped him forge ahead during some of the most challenging days of his life.

He smiled, with a reflective gaze as he carefully chose his words. I could practically *feel* the playback of the memories in his mind. He turned to me and said, "Christopher, the wheel of leadership was first chiseled centuries ago. And yet, we always need to adjust and adapt as leaders. Times change. People change. The constant we must always remember is: in leadership, people come first."

I find myself thinking of the wisdom he shared each day. It's the secret to building high-performing teams and thriving organizations.

As we look ahead at the modern business landscape, a people-first approach now takes center stage. How we communicate and connect with our employees and customers will define our future success. The rules of engagement in the workplace have changed. Technology is evolving at warp speed. So is where and how we work. The need to collaborate effectively is essential for championing the success of high-performing teams. But with the only certainty in the future being uncertainty, the question on the mind of every leader and organization is now: How will we continue to adapt?

Organizations and employees are learning to adjust to the new normal of remote and hybrid environments, while leaders and their teams are trying to find alignment on expectations. Employees feel disconnected from their senior leaders. Middle managers are finding it more challenging to keep up with the pace of work, while finding time to manage their teams.

The top human resources issues facing businesses are hiring, employee engagement, and retention, yet many organizations are struggling to build authentic connection with their employees. Leaders must focus their time and energy on supporting their people, or they risk watching them exit for better opportunities.

To be a champion leader, an emotionally intelligent approach is what is needed for this new business era. Emotional intelligence (EQ) helps accelerate the speed of your performance to build the needed connection with your organization and customers. It's through this invaluable skill set that we connect with ourselves and bring our self-awareness, motivation, and empathy outward to build emotional connection with others. Doing this is the greatest investment you can make in growing your leadership skills and supporting the people of your organization.

When leaders personalize relationships, show their employees they care, and dedicate the time to support their development, bottom-line profits soar, as reported in "The Impact of Employee Engagement on Performance" by the *Harvard Business Review* Analytic Services.[1] People choose to not only stick around, but also put more energy and passion into their work when they feel valued.

The ripple effects show a more motivated workforce that feels greater connection to the company mission and to their leadership. Every touchpoint they have with your customers—and prospective customers—is more enthusiastic and positive in nature.

Emotionally intelligent leadership is about being the best we can for ourselves and then being the best we can for the people we lead.

It's about igniting passion and belief in our organization, which helps solve problems and leads to the development of our team members. Through empathy and curiosity, we gain insights into the heartbeat of our organization—our people—and then connect that back to our strategic goals.

Putting People First for Better Organizational Results

The people-first model is what creates longevity and long-term profit. As legendary Southwest Airlines founder and CEO Herb Kelleher said: "Honor, respect, care for, protect, and reward your employees—regardless of title or position. And in turn, they will treat each other, and their external customers, in a warm, in a caring, and in a hospitable way. This causes external customers to return."[2]

Kelleher walked his talk. Southwest Airlines experienced 47 consecutive years of profitability from 1973 to 2020—a jaw-dropping feat in the highly competitive airline industry. But it wasn't *just* for the quality of their peanuts. Southwest Airlines was a company built on prioritizing the needs and wants of its people from the inside out. It's why they experienced the astonishing success that they did.

It's time for organizations and leaders to understand what emotional intelligence is, why it matters, and how this skill set can be instilled throughout your organization for maximum benefit. EQ will be the key differentiator in high performance over the long haul. It's a skill set that every individual can learn and improve on each day. The need for emotional intelligence in communicating effectively, collaborating, and driving results is critical in all industries. It's this focus on soft skills that is essential for the modern workforce.

As new research comes in, we continue to see how emotional intelligence threads its way through the most desirable labor market skills.

Take this remarkable insight from Pearson, for example:[3]

Our study analyzed labor market trends in four major economies—US, UK, Australia, and Canada—and confirms that, while technical skills remain highly valued, the top five most sought-after skills . . . are all human skills:

- *Communication*
- *Customer Service*
- *Leadership*
- *Attention to Detail*
- *Collaboration*

These attributes are part of what form the composite skill set of emotional intelligence and are the cornerstone of a champion leader. As vital as leadership, collaboration, and connection are today, the need for these soft skills will continue to grow stronger. This is what I'm told each day in conversation by leaders and executives. It's what I'm observing firsthand while working with organizations to help bridge the communication gap between executive leadership and middle managers, which affects the relationship between line managers and front-line employees.

There is a burning need for leaders and employees—at all levels—who can communicate effectively. Creating connection means going deeper than the surface level; it's about how you empathize, gain understanding, and truly help your employees and coworkers to become the best versions of themselves.

Building a Modern, Authentic Culture to Benefit Employees

As one generation of employees exits the workforce and a newer generation enters, we're seeing how the needs and wants of employees have changed. In particular, millennials and Gen Z employees are looking for greater connection to their leaders and better work-life balance. All employees are signaling a desire for more career development and growth opportunities within their organization. This has moved multigenerational communication to the forefront of leadership focus, as leaders seek to reach and build relationships across all levels. Attributes such as self-awareness, empathy, and mastering the art of social skill carry immense value for how leaders build connection.

So what's at stake? The future of your organization. Your ability to advance your career in the direction of where you truly want it to go. The well-being and betterment of every person whose life you have the profound ability to touch. There are more employees than ever before who are dissatisfied with the status quo. They're quiet quitting, or giving the minimum amount of effort each day because they don't feel recognized or appreciated. They're daydreaming about better job opportunities.

Championship leadership connection revitalizes organizations. Hygiene factors such as pay, title, and work flexibility will always hold sway. But it's care and *connection* that empower the efforts of the organization by building relationships that are personalized, engaging, and genuine. This is how you foster trust and retain the best people in your organization. It's also how you establish an open dialogue that's receptive to feedback.

The most powerful pieces of feedback I see consistently when conducting 360° leadership assessments are the following:

1. *I wish my leader took the time to get to know me and our team better on a personal level.*
2. *I wish my leader shared more about herself or himself with me and our team.*

What conclusions can we draw from this? After all, this is a business, not a social club, right? Yes, but the bottom line is that many employees are now looking for leaders who are willing to ditch superficial relationships in favor of going all-in to forge authentic ones. A lack of engagement and connectedness is at the heart of what's caused many people to flee organizations in droves. The modern workforce wants leaders who respect them, value their contributions, and embrace optimism and candor. Shifting to a positive, connected way of leading will help you retain your top talent and build a cohesive, caring culture that achieves dynamic results.

Solidifying Your Champion Leader Foundation

The mindset of a champion leader is rooted in emotional intelligence, which increases self-awareness while enhancing your strengths. When you have fortified your leadership core, you can cultivate a personalized, transformational leadership experience for others. You'll be able to inspire and commit to positively influencing your team members to create an impact of their own.

The foundation of every transformational connection is inspired by the Golden Rule: it's the desire to treat someone else the way you'd want to be treated in return. By helping each individual, you are simultaneously building a culture that seeks to elevate each person in the organization. Being a supporter isn't enough anymore. It won't cut it in this new era of business. Champion leaders are needed. There's far too much at stake in this hypercompetitive workforce with millions of employees leaving organizations to find better fits for their personal and professional needs.

A recent Harris Poll showed that: "Over half of employees want to leave [their jobs]. . . ." One of the reasons was that employees "felt that their employers did not understand them, that they weren't providing empathy."[4] (The other reason was work flexibility.)

This is the pain and reality employers are dealing with. Maybe you know the feeling.

I encourage you to lead with empathy and listen to your employees' needs. Leaders need to get in touch with their emotional sides to find the champion within. Leaders who identify what their employees need and want—and then engage and deliver—will be able to retain top performers and set up their organizations for long-term success. This need to evolve and adapt to changing demands is a central component of achieving success.

I also implore you to put in the work and think about what kind of leader you are today—and the one you aspire to be tomorrow. Throughout these pages, there are exercises that will equip you with the tools to do so, as well as questions to help you reflect on your journey. Champion leaders have a learner's mindset that is always seeking to grow and improve. By making sense of your experiences, you'll evolve each day into more of the version of yourself that you want to become.

Your Playbook for Emotionally Intelligent Leadership

The Champion Leader is your playbook for building a culture of connected relationships that bring everyone closer together and united toward achieving your organizational goals. As we transition further away from the conventional nine-to-five work environment, it's this all-around cognizance and selfless leadership that will have a transformational effect on your culture.

This book is for leaders at all levels—in all industries—who seek to advance their emotional intelligence skill set and grow into becoming the best versions of themselves. You'll gain insights from a broad range of leaders, from those operating on the global scale to leaders positively influencing their local communities at the grassroots level. There are vivid, powerful stories that will help you visualize what you might do if faced with similar situations.

Chapters 1–9, 11, and 12 feature:

- An opening story filled with leadership lessons and practical ways to use emotional intelligence to your advantage;
- Four questions to help you better reflect on your past journey, as well as your future personal aspirations and professional goals;
- A leadership exercise filled with tools to help reinforce your learning and make it truly actionable; and
- A "champion's checklist" to help guide you through each new season of change.

Chapter 10, however, is filled with unique wisdom and vibes. Focusing on "the little things" that truly matter in leadership, the text marches to a different beat than the other chapters. It features "the voice of the leader" with powerful, real-life reflections from five experts in their fields.

The "Champion's Watch" section is both an homage to a wonderful man, and an inspirational call to lead from the heart.

The "Leadership Resources" section will help provide additional guidance on how to continue your champion's journey.

Championship leadership works to create connection and trust, which are the bedrock of leadership. While it may seem counterintuitive, to build trust you need to be bold and assertive. You need to take risks, dare to innovate, and adapt to change. Take these risks with your team. Be there *in it* with them through it all. Model the leadership you want to see in others and go all-in. You'll earn their respect and create an enduring partnership.

High-performing teams and organizations will thrive or fail based on the power of their people—the coming together of individuals to form a high-functioning unit whose values, purpose, and goals are far greater than the sum of its parts. But remember, the secret of every high-performing team is the ability of each individual to maximize their talents and skills and contribute for the benefit of all.

The time is now to start leading like a champion. This change begins with you. Become the best leader you can be and help others become the best that they can be.

As we embark on this exciting journey together, let's focus on the words of the great Herb Kelleher: "The business of business is people. Yesterday, today, and forever."[5]

Chapter 1

Leadership Connection Perfection (*Lead with Emotional Intelligence and Bring People Together to Achieve Incredible Results*)

"Psychic satisfaction is what employees and even external customers are primarily seeking."

—Herb Kelleher

At the dawn of my business career, I began working in finance at the corner of Wall Street and Broad Street in Lower Manhattan looking to learn about stocks, bonds, and everything in between. I was an intern for one of the largest specialist firms on the floor of the New York Stock Exchange (NYSE). I fell in love with the close-knit environment, the jokes, the importance of every moment, and the incredible speed at which the job moved. In at 8:30, finished by market close at 4 p.m.—and those 7.5 hours felt like a New York minute.

I learned early on what makes the millions of speedy transactions worth billions of dollars every day work: human beings. Despite all the technological advances of how orders were placed and deals closed, at its core, it was a people business that attracted me. People communicating with other people and relying on each other. Understanding the rhythm, body language, and pace of work.

After I graduated college, I came back to interview for a job with the same specialist firm. I was eager to embark on what I hoped would be a long career in New York finance. I met one of the partners for lunch and had a great conversation. I connected well with everyone the previous summer and earned their respect by being eager to learn and to take on new tasks. But there was a palpable feeling in the air that the times were a-changin'. The US economy was entering into a recession. Compounding things, the NASDAQ and electronic trading markets were gaining traction over the traditional NYSE. Which meant less people, more computers.

I finished up my meeting and we both exited the restaurant onto Exchange Place in the shadows of the iconic statue of George Washington that overlooks Wall Street. The partner shook my hand and let me know he'd be following up and hoped that things would work out. It was then that he turned to me and said words I've never forgotten. He said, "Christopher, *this* will never, ever go away" (and he paused for a moment). "Despite the economy, despite the markets becoming more electronic, there will always be a need for face-to-face interactions. This whole operation works because of conversations, negotiations, and people. This business always has been and always will be about you and me. This all works because of people."

When it comes down to brass tacks, every business is truly about people. No matter how far artificial intelligence, quantum computing, and new technological innovations advance, the critical skills of communication, collaboration, and relationship building will always make the difference in business. Connection is sparked when you choose to build dynamic relationships. Dynamic relationships are formed by emotionalizing the way you connect and doing so with authenticity, assertiveness, candor, and empathy. This matters in driving results. It matters in generating ideas and innovating. And it sure matters in building a culture of connection that leads to high-performing teams.

When you focus on improving and enhancing these skills throughout your leadership journey, you make an investment in the skills of the future that will carry you further into a career of success and fulfillment.

The Connection Success Formula: Empathy + Candor + Authenticity + Assertiveness = Victory

It's easy for us to think that our industry, job, or specific company is a unicorn. "No one does things the way we do here!" I hear it on a regular basis. Every organization has its idiosyncrasies, embedded habits, and culture that make it unique from everyone else. That's because every person is unique and brings their own values, beliefs, thoughts, and ideas with them to work each day. But there's one unifying thread I've observed that transcends industries, jobs, and organizations: the ability to communicate effectively and combine that with a desire to build enduring relationships.

This connection success formula was developed over 20 years of direct experience coaching, consulting, and working with the most accomplished global leaders representing Fortune 500 companies and leading organizations. It's backed by research and neuroscience that shows our human tendency and desire toward wanting to build meaningful relationships in an effort to collaborate on accomplishing things. I've found this to be a universal framework that works in every organization and is best grafted on our own emotionally intelligent leadership style to form connection with people.

Organizational results are always achieved because of effective communication. Without it, there would be no team. Every innovation, project, and task begins with an idea, which is backed by discipline, strategy—a plan—and is then understood and communicated to others to make it possible. The starting point for communication is listening. Someone needs to be on the receiving end of the great idea, strategy, or next step in the process. Our goal as leaders should be to want to inspire and influence others to listen and connect with our ideas. We should lead first with listening to others. This reciprocal communication loop is the beginning of creating practical understanding and emotional resonance. It's the beginning of connection.

The tact we use, and emotional connection that we create, matters in how we aim to influence both ourselves and others. I know leaders who spend sleepless nights thinking about what motivates their employees. The truth is, it really does come back to recognizing, showing appreciation, and meaningfully taking action on feedback provided by employees. It's exactly what STARZ president and CEO Jeffrey Hirsch told me: "When you're managing everyone to truly understand people as individuals, to know what drives them, to understand what's at stake for them, you can then tailor your ability to lead them. Building this connection improves the employee experience for everyone."[1]

It improves well-being.

When HR leaders were asked what they're prioritizing in 2023 to engage and retain talent, a whopping 59% responded employee well-being, 52% said increased flexibility with where/when employees work, and 39% responded recognition and rewards. This same report established "the #1 driver of connection" to be recognition.[2] Connected leadership means being present for the people you lead.

Modern leaders invest time in building relationships that are formed on a foundation of *authenticity*. They take the lead and initiate conversations by being *assertive* in communicating their thoughts and intentional in receiving the message of someone else. I like to say this is what it means to go all-in when communicating with people. This leadership connection perfection is made possible with *candor*, which means speaking from the heart, without ego, and with a sincere desire to connect with the other person. This requires *empathy*, which is the willingness to understand someone else from their own perspective, and to listen without bias, with care, and genuine focus.

Let's begin first with empathy, which is often misunderstood and undervalued. Empathy isn't about being passive. It's not reserved only for certain settings or people. Empathy is one of the most powerful leadership qualities and a hallmark of emotional intelligence (EQ). Unlocking its greatness is at the core of building an emotionally intelligent culture.

Empathy

Empathy is the ability to understand, perceive, or feel what someone is going through from within their frame of reference. Or simply put, to put ourselves in someone else's shoes. When you invest in someone's personal and professional interests, you gain an understanding of them. They gain greater respect for your leadership. Safra Catz, CEO of Oracle, is an empathetic leader who places a high value on each employee's unique contributions, ideas, and skills. She's a clear, transparent communicator who takes the time to listen and understand people. She's created an environment at Oracle that is diverse, inclusive, and welcoming to each individual's talents and viewpoints. She recognizes leadership begins with focusing on each individual.

The Greater Good Science Center at the University of California-Berkeley breaks empathy into two areas:[3]

- "Affective empathy" refers to the sensations and feelings we get in response to others' emotions; this can include mirroring what that person is feeling or just feeling stressed when we detect another's fear or anxiety.
- "Cognitive empathy," sometimes called "perspective taking," refers to our ability to identify and understand other people's emotions.

The importance of "putting ourselves in someone else's shoes" is not lost on any of us. My goal here is to point out the tremendous impact this can have as it pertains to building connection. The best way to understand this is to recognize the challenges many companies are dealing with.

Two of the most important issues organizations are dealing with today are burnout and employee engagement. Employees feel disconnected from their leaders and managers. They're not having frequent conversations about well-being and feedback; most conversations are focused on day-to-day tasks and can lack a human element. Many employees are maintaining an unrealistic, fast-break pace of long hours, without any signs of it ending. So what can you do about it?

First, it's critical for leaders to create a space for conversations—and to ensure those conversations actually take place. In my work with leaders, I encourage them to focus on two aspects of communication: quality and frequency. This starts in one-on-one meetings with planned, structured touchpoints. It's reinforced by the moments throughout the week where managers and direct reports can briefly connect on tasks, personal matters, or personnel-related matters. Empathy is what increases the probability that these conversations take place because it's always showing care, concern, and devotion toward the needs of the person you're communicating with.

Second, think of empathy as the bond that holds relationships together and enables them to have longevity through the years. When it comes to connection, you're wise to listen first, then ask questions, and then if it makes sense, provide your perspective or advice.

To be truly empathetic, you need to be self-aware. You must understand and recognize that people want to feel heard, be respected, and be treated fairly. Asking open-ended questions helps you to gain understanding. You can start by checking in with someone and asking, "What's on your mind?" or "What are ways I can help?" Empathy is also about going deeper. It's about getting beyond the surface level and creating impact in how you connect and support someone. The secret of empathy is to lead with curiosity and passion toward wanting to get to know someone on both a personal and professional level.

This means showing up with positive body language and being your authentic self (I talk more about authenticity later in this chapter). In other words: just be you. Start with kindness and gratitude in conversations with your teams. Recognize and point out something they've done well. Focus not just on results but on their attitude and effort in the process. Listen with full presence and intent. Eliminate distractions and aim to learn from them. Listen with purpose by maintaining eye contact, good posture, and focus. Don't listen with the desire to get your next word in edgewise and don't look as if you literally only have one minute. People will be able to tell and could privately question your motives. What really matters is how they see the way you value your time with them.

Championship leadership focuses on helping others and leading with a big heart to reach solutions that benefit everyone. Empathy plays a huge role in this, and it's about giving of yourself to someone else. You should seek to understand first why you're spending the time you are to connect, how you want to help someone succeed, and how this makes both you and your organization better.

Only then can you positively influence the people around you. The outer work begins with the inner work. Thoughtful leadership focuses on connection that shows care for someone's well-being. It's guided by the belief that someone will be better off because you listened and supported them.

Think about the positive ripple effects that you can create in someone's life! Think about if you were to be there to support other people in your organization. You never really know just how much your words and actions can affect someone else. And what's challenging is, they won't always tell you. But do it anyway. Encourage and motivate your employees. Be there to support people on their teams and with cross-functional partners—that's the next step for how you make an impact on someone else. Promote a culture where people come together to connect, not where people live in fear of sharing ideas.

Reflection questions for empathy:

- How have you shown care and concern toward others in your organization?
- Do you listen first, or do you focus on wanting to say what's on your mind?
- What will help you listen with greater presence in each moment?
- How do you want someone to feel after they've interacted with you?

Ultimately, empathy should lead to the desire to show and feel a *champion's* connection to someone else, displaying a genuine desire of care and the spirit to want to help someone. This means that we support someone by clearly understanding their needs and wants and being there for them at every stage of their growth and development. Former PepsiCo CEO Indra Nooyi once said: "You need to be able to look at that person and say, 'I value you as a person. I know that you have a life beyond PepsiCo, and I'm going to respect you for your entire life, not just treat you as employee number 4,567.'"[4]

At its core, empathy creates a bridge to compassion and understanding for your people. When they know you're invested in them, they will truly want to return the favor by performing to the best of their ability.

Candor

In the summer of 2022, the world's largest talent agency was on the verge of a significant change. They were about to appoint two new leaders to oversee the agency. William Morris Endeavor (WME) needed new leadership to create mutually beneficial relationships. They were looking for someone to *connect* and unify business units throughout the agency. They also wanted to change the perception of how both current and future clients saw the agency. Christian Muirhead and Richard Weitz were hired to fill the roles as co-chairmen.

What Weitz realized very early on was how important transparency and openness would be both in how he and Muirhead communicated with their internal employees and in the service extended to current and prospective clients. When it comes to superior customer service, it's the *little things*, or the small details, which really aren't so small.

The first thing Weitz told the agents and leaders at their annual summit was that clients would no longer wait on hold when calling to speak with someone. He learned from conversations, because he's an agent himself, that sometimes clients were waiting for minutes at a time to speak with someone. If that call was unanswered, the wait time could last for hours—even days. Some clients parted ways with WME because they felt ignored. It was clear to Weitz that they left because they weren't feeling the personal touch that means everything in the entertainment business.

As a result, he completely revamped their customer service model to ensure a more personalized touch would take place. Qualities such as *empathy* and *candor* would take prominence and form the foundation for WME's leadership approach.

Clients do not wait on hold. Period.

Weitz reasoned that if clients are the lifeblood of our agency, then we must treat them like royalty. That treatment begins with extending candor, sincerely expressing a desire to help, and providing top-notch customer service at every touchpoint.

When you communicate to everyone in your organization that your chief purpose is helping others, you are creating a culture of connection. To truly put your customers first, begin *locally* with the candor and kindness you direct toward your own employees. This creates a reciprocal relationship of first-class service and communications that is unbeatable.

Candor is delivered in the feedback you provide your people. Speaking candidly, one thing that drives me crazy is when I hear a leader begin a feedback conversation like this:

> *You did a really great job on this. But there are several things that I think could make it better. . .*

And then, brace yourself. Because those "several things" could feel like a thousand. It's always best to play things straight. Candor is the opposite of passive-aggressive communication. Passive-aggressiveness creates ill will, hesitancy, and indecision. Candor cuts through red tape with precision and gets you directly to the point. You want to eliminate as many barriers as you can to communicating effectively, which is the whole point of candor. Start simple. Honestly. Communication begins with listening. The best communication is candid and simple. As Leonardo da Vinci once said, "Simplicity is the ultimate sophistication."

You can do this by giving people honest, sincere guidance on how they're doing and how you, your leaders, and your managers are in a position to help them. Enable a culture where one-on-one meetings take place regularly between every manager and their direct reports. Empower every manager to provide feedback, and allow employees to own part of the meeting agenda. That could be related to career development, professional development, or an opportunity to offer innovative ideas on better ways to do things. Remember: it comes back to listening for managers. Provide feedback and listen to their ideas, thoughts, and feedback. Always be in a position to help.

This is empowered by sincere, open communications that genuinely show you care!

Help can come in a variety of ways. We often hear, "Let me know if I can help you" or "If I can help you in any way, please let me know." That's a great place to start. But go further. Candid, connected leadership is informed on *how* to help. This ability to know and understand certainly takes time. It takes conscious effort. It comes from the little conversations within the day that add up to be highly informed conversations over time. Highly informed conversations lead to healthy, connected relationships.

I want to ask you now to take a moment to put yourself in the shoes of someone you lead. I realize that might mean going back to earlier in your career. And I want you to ask yourself the following questions as if you are them reflecting with self-awareness and clear eyes.

Reflection questions for candor:

- How would I feel if my leader only checked in on me when my work was finished?
- How would I feel if my leader only came to me with bad news?
- How would I feel if my leader—or a team member—always treated me passive-aggressively?
- How would I feel if my leader never asked me how I was doing and didn't make an effort to help me develop and achieve my goals?

That would feel very transactional, wouldn't it? And with even a minute of reflection, is that the culture or the "brand" of leadership that you'd want to cultivate?

Candor isn't easy. It requires trust, discipline, and attention to detail. It requires that we give someone the attention they deserve by communicating in a way that lets them know we've got their best interests at heart.

Authenticity

There's an incredible moment in the movie *A Beautiful Day in the Neighborhood* with Tom Hanks that lives at the intersection of who we are and who we want to be. If you haven't seen the film, the plot focuses on a journalist seeking to interview Fred Rogers (you and I may know him better as Mister Rogers) for an *Esquire* magazine front page spread about heroes. The New York–based journalist, who's incredibly cynical, travels to Pittsburgh to ask him questions at the WQED studio. He tells Fred Rogers that he's writing a piece about heroes. He asks him, "Do you consider yourself a hero?" to which Fred Rogers says he does not. Then the writer (played by Matthew Rhys) asks him, "What about Mister Rogers, is he a hero?" and Tom Hanks shakes his head, and says, "I . . . I don't understand the question."

The writer grins and says, "Well, there's you (pause), Fred . . . and then there's the character you play, Mister Rogers."

And the camera pans back to Tom Hanks, who sits there (I counted!) for four seconds, which feels like an eternity. He calmly stares at the reporter and deftly chooses not to answer the question. Instead, he asks the journalist a question related to a previous part of the conversation.

The incredible acting by both men, Hanks in particular, is on display. The insinuation is that Fred Rogers and the character that he played for the PBS television program *Mister Rogers' Neighborhood* were one and the same. He was simply recording that on television for all of us to watch and learn as we ate our cheddar cheese Goldfish and drank apple juice from our sippy cups.

Fred Rogers *was* Mister Rogers. Mister Rogers *was* Fred Rogers. And we felt that authenticity.

Now, I don't think you spend part of your days recording public access television programs for children—like I said, I don't think! The real you—the champion leader in you—is best served to show up authentically, whether the cameras are rolling or not, and no matter who's watching.

The real you is someone highly self-aware of their strengths, someone who is clear on what they're trying to achieve and is able to articulate that vision to others. You show up and lead with values. You cultivate belief and hope and lift up your people in the process. What they see is what they get with you. While you can tailor the way you communicate to each individual to meet them where they're at, you will always treat everyone with kindness, respect, and courtesy. You follow through on your words and actions. That sense of professional and personal responsibility is what earns the respect of everyone.

Character and Reputation

Legendary basketball coach John Wooden once said, "Be more concerned with your character than your reputation, for your character is what you really are, while your reputation is merely what others think you to be." When you're authentic, honest, open, real, and seeking to help others—while driving business results to get done—everyone will know that. They will honor and respect you for that. And your customers—both current and future—will want to do business with this high-character individual and organization that treats people with integrity—the way they'd love to be treated.

Authenticity is one of the most valuable leadership traits because it builds connection and creates transformational organizations. I've observed authenticity—and a lack thereof—in over 20 years of professional work. When authenticity is there, everyone knows it. People feel free to be themselves.

The term "fake it till you make it" only works for so long before people catch on. The way to lead is to establish a rock-solid foundation of values, beliefs, purpose, and goals and then do your best to influence and instill them throughout your organization—with the participation and help of your people.

Bring people along with you for the journey. Form authentic connections by coming as you are—showing up as your true self, without ego and with sincerity. That will create an inclusive culture where people know they can then show up as their true selves. I'm always amazed by how much people underestimate authenticity as a core leadership trait. There's a lot of wasted time in business spent trying to be like someone else. Take the time to think and reflect on the way you want to show up each day as a leader. Then, commit to doing it. As Kurt Cobain famously sang, "Come as you are."

Reflection questions for authenticity:

- What qualities or activities help you to show up as your true self each day?
- What values have you chosen as your foundation to help guide and anchor you?
- What is the most meaningful feedback you've received about your character?
- How would your closest colleagues describe you as a person? As a leader?

Pressures

My favorite definition of "authentic" is, "representing one's true nature or beliefs; true to oneself or to the person identified."[5] So what can affect us and prevent us from showing up authentically in our business lives?

- **Fear:** We fear letting people see us as who we really are. We fear tough conversations. We can be afraid of sharing disappointing news with a colleague, so we avoid these situations.
- **Social pressure:** We don't listen to our intuition and instead cave to what we think others might want or expect from us—even when it doesn't feel right.
- **Mental chess:** This can be a competitive mental game we play with ourselves, thinking we should be at a particular point of achievement or that we should follow the path of someone else, when we're best served to focus on our own path forward.
- **Impostor syndrome:** The opposite of self-assurance, this is when self-doubt enters our minds and makes us think our skills or accomplishments aren't adequate. Simply put, we think we're not doing well, when we are. It's critical to cultivate self-confidence to counteract impostor syndrome (see Chapter 2). Pursue feedback and external validation from others, but remember, internal validation is best. There will always be external pressures in business. Avoid putting too much pressure on yourself. While putting some pressure on yourself can be a motivational driver, putting too much can rob you of your confidence and lead to a pressure-packed cycle of stress and self-doubt. At worst, it can make you feel like you're someone that you're not. Be clear on exactly what you're striving to do.

Think about it—where does too much pressure really get you? It might be blocking you from being your most authentic self and leader. We're at our best when we stand out from the rest, not when we try to conform. It's why Oscar Wilde's quote, "Be yourself; everyone else is already taken," serves as enduring wisdom.

In relationships, we can sniff a fake or an inauthentic person a mile away. I've found that the more we concern ourselves with our character and stay true to our beliefs, the more we grow and become a better person in the process. To act in an authentic manner, we must first give deep thought to what we're trying to do and how we're aiming to help others. This requires keen emotional intelligence, which is partially composed of the ever-powerful trait of self-awareness. Be mindful of your thoughts. Be careful of how your actions influence others. Act with good intentions and motives, and you'll model authenticity.

Assertiveness

Several years ago I was coaching the COO of a virtual health care services company, helping him in his transition to the organization. He shared with me one practice that he firmly believed in, which I had experienced earlier in my career as an employee. He told me it was critically important for him to show up at the monthly new employee orientation day to get to know each new hire.

This happened 12 days per year. Maybe for a total of 12 hours.

He'd come to answer questions, provide a tour of the office, and be a visible resource to let new employees know he was there for them. He provided them with his contact information and encouraged them to reach out if he could make their journeys better. In the time he was there, he said retention improved at the company by 50%. Coincidence? I think not.

Let me first explain what I mean about being assertive. To be truly assertive, we must have a foundation of self-awareness. This means knowing what we want to say and do, and then acting to positively influence and help someone. Assertive leaders have positive body language and tailor how they communicate to each person or audience. They speak with confidence and conviction. Ask someone about their time at your company, where they live, their hobbies, and be there to listen. Then, you can offer ways to help. And follow through.

The best time to build a relationship is now. At first, that may begin with small talk. Here's the thing—small talk won't work for some people. And you might be thinking to yourself, *I can't stand small talk!* Reframing the way you see it—and the connection that comes from initiating the conversation—is essential.

To connect with someone for the first time, we need an entry point. I've found in thousands of coaching conversations that it's often not someone's fear of small talk. It's mostly about summoning the courage to start the conversation. You don't have to lead with the weather. And you certainly don't need a green screen nor a meteorologist's expert understanding of cold fronts, bomb cyclones, or cumulonimbus clouds. Here are some entry points or topics to lead with:

- How someone is doing/feeling;
- How their family/partner is doing;
- The weekend;
- Popular TV show;
- What's going on in their neighborhood;
- Their favorite restaurant; or
- What they're most passionate about.

Take the game to them. Feel empowered to play offense. Share some of these answers for yourself. We never quite know how someone perceives us; there could be some intimidation there, and they may be waiting for you to open up to them.

Reflection questions for assertiveness:

- How are you holding people accountable to goals and results?
- How often do you initiate conversations to get to know your team better?
- Are you an advocate for yourself? For your team's ideas? Their accomplishments?
- What's one outside-the-box idea you can use to better get to know people on your team—and in your organization?

Being assertive means showing up with confidence, self-assurance, and purpose in the way you clearly communicate with others. Assertiveness is also about conflict resolution and knowing when to mediate a conversation that will solve a problem to help people move forward with clarity.

Assertive leaders are self-advocates and advocates for others. Be willing to advocate for what you want. Be an advocate and champion for the feedback and ideas that come from your employees. Quite like recognizing and showing appreciation for your employees will lead to cohesion and belonging, advocating for their ideas—and helping to bring them to life—will build a wellspring of goodwill and support from your team.

Assertiveness comes back to conviction in your beliefs, knowing what to say no to, and standing firm for your team's vision, values, and mission. Assertiveness means being unafraid to delegate work and responsibilities to others because it empowers people in your organization and gives them purpose. It means that you're focused on thinking strategically and spending more time in that space to better support your team by gaining support from others.

One example of an assertive leader is Fidelity CEO Abby Johnson, one of the most powerful financial leaders in the world. She said, "I demand pretty aggressive goal setting and a commitment to measured progress towards those goals."[6] It's a revealing insight into the mind of a leader who is willing to hold people to a high standard of accountability, while also asking a lot of questions. As a leader, be willing to hold your team to a high standard. Initiate conversations to evaluate what's gone well and what hasn't.

Assertiveness supports creative thinking and effective communication. It allows you to build relationships without ego while respecting others, seeking connection, and finding mutually beneficial solutions.

Emotionalizing Your Connection

When we can see someone's authenticity, feel their empathy, respect their assertiveness, and process their candor, we realize we're not just carrying out a transaction or purchasing a good or service from someone—we're engaged in something transformational beyond time and money spent.

Emotionalizing your connection means going beyond business as usual and creating an experience that people leave feeling fulfilled, happy, and yes, even rewarded from having participated in. It may mean bringing in a coffee for a colleague on a rainy Wednesday morning when they're sleep-deprived. This could show up in how you welcome someone new to your team, and ask them how they're adjusting. Connection perfection is often in the small details—the moments throughout the day and small conversations—where an attention to detail and mindfulness for others is everything.

Connection inspires the "magnetic moments" that help teams come together to achieve dynamic results. Here's what it looks like to reveal authentic pieces of yourself in an effort to create belonging:

> *"We just rode our bikes over the Golden Gate Bridge to Sausalito this past weekend."*
>
> *"Oh yeah? We did that last month and stopped for ice cream when we got there."*
>
> *"That's awesome!"*

All of a sudden, there's a spark. There's energy. A door just opened that may have otherwise remained shut. Champion leaders have photographic memories. They remember these magnetic moments and recall them in future conversations. You have the ability to drill deeper into personal connections and to take a chance by putting yourself out there in a way that's vulnerable and real.

Listen first. We're all going to spend a lot of time with our colleagues. You're so much more likely to experience success, happiness, and fulfillment when you build an emotional bond of support and respect. It's going to bring you closer together, open up clearer lines of communication, and inspire greater desire in others.

No one is saying you have to go out for happy hour drinks with your team every month. No one is saying you have to binge-watch hours of a Netflix show with your colleague. But if you can build a shared trust built on respect, affection, esteem, and shared activities, the bond will develop to want to sacrifice and help one another. It creates a stronger feeling of team, rather than *I'm here for me*. Bonds are formed through a promotion of social interaction and efforts to get to know your team.

A Gallup study showed "employees who feel as though their manager is invested in them as *people* are more likely to be engaged."[7] I encourage you to go beyond the superficial:

- Create a psychologically safe (more on this in Chapter 6) environment for people to share ideas and ask questions. As a leader, your goal should be to inspire an emotionalized feeling that creates powerful trust.
- Share how you feel.
- Do something nice and unexpected for someone.
- Apologize when you make a mistake and seek forgiveness (humility and integrity).

Connect Like TED

There's evidence for how we can emotionally connect with people. Carmine Gallo wrote about this in his book, *Talk Like Ted.* He analyzed over 500 of the most popular TED talks of all time. He found that successful TED speakers spent 65% of their talks emotionalizing their connection with the audience through storytelling or *pathos*; 25% occurred through *logos*, or reason, which is often backed by statistics or evidence; and 10% was through *ethos*, or character and credibility.

Think about that: nearly two-thirds of the speaker's time was spent telling stories that created an emotional connection. Why? Because it's *real.* It's engaging, and it helps us to relate to people.

Throughout thousands of hours of leadership coaching conversations, direct experience, and research, I've found the way we connect with our teams is no different. Emotional connection isn't just a "nice to have." Emotionalizing the way we connect is the best way to build high-performing teams. It helps you build a bond of trust that leads to successful outcomes.

So I ask again: How do you want someone to feel after they've interacted with you?

Leadership Connection Perfection Exercise

Set up a social connection opportunity each month with your team members. This can take place virtually or (ideally) in-person. The purpose of this is not to focus on work tasks or projects. This is set up to get to know each other better. Share pieces of yourself, introduce a musical artist you like or a meme you found funny. Get to know another team member and keep it casual and non-work related. Have fun with it! Mix in a question such as "What's your go-to emoji, and why?" Remember to tell stories. Storytelling is how we build emotional connection.

Champion's Checklist (Tools and Takeaways)

☑ Be proactive, not reactive, in how you communicate and resolve conflict.

☑ Always prioritize in-person connection, and make every effort to get to know each person on your team.

☑ Eliminate passive-aggressive language; be assertive, but be kind and respectful.

☑ Always go to someone directly, one-on-one, when looking to clear things up.

☑ Listen to your team. You'll be surprised how much they'll open up to you.

Source: Christopher D. Connors

Chapter 2

You (*Championship Leadership Starts with Mastering Self-Awareness*)

"I think self-awareness is probably the most important thing towards being a champion."

—Billie Jean King

"You'll know the difference."

Four of the most meaningful words I've ever heard.

During my college years, I served as the sports director of the NPR-member radio station that doubled as our campus radio station. It was a hands-on experience unmatched for any 18–22-year-old student, calling play-by-play for college sports games, doling out assignments, and elevating my fellow students to do great work. One of the best parts of the job was the road trips. We'd nosh on tasty food, meet interesting people, and share hilarious stories. We traveled around the country to broadcast road games and be the eyes and ears for thousands of people listening in on the radio and Internet. One road trip in particular will always hold a special place in my memory.

We were traveling back from a lacrosse game played at Penn State University. I was replaying the game broadcast in my mind, as

I usually did, thinking of what went well and what I could've done better. I felt I was doing a pretty good job broadcasting the games. I'd often get kind praise from my dad, who always found a way to tune in. But I figured, That's my dad. I wanted to know what my manager, and oftentimes broadcast partner, thought. He was the general manager of the radio station, a veteran of NPR and college broadcasting, and an incredibly talented audio professional with quite the broadcasting résumé. Michael Black was a caring man, dedicated to his craft, and someone from whom I learned a great deal.

I was shy by nature, and yet I finally mustered up the courage to ask him for feedback on how he felt I did on the game broadcast. I wanted to know how I was doing so I could improve, and I figured a good compliment or two wouldn't hurt either.

As we traveled north through the early spring night in rural Pennsylvania, he said words that caught me by surprise but taught me the most powerful lesson in self-awareness I've ever learned. He turned from the driver seat, gazed at me, and said, "I'm not always going to tell you when you're doing well. But I will tell you when you mess up. You'll know the difference."

I knew right away that it was a special moment of reckoning. I felt entrusted with the freedom of thought and intuition that every employee—and person—craves. It was Michael Black's way of telling a young man that the beauty of the journey is figuring it out, learning and growing along the way. *Knowing the difference* is the prize we earn from self-awareness. Strengthening our self-awareness muscles allows us to recognize and understand who we are, how we're doing, and how to improve.

Self-awareness is informed by feedback, positive or constructive. The nuance is in knowing, exploring, and digging deeper based on our own analysis. Michael Black was a champion leader—laid-back, caring, charming, and authentically himself. He let me mess up.

Heck, he let me fall flat on my face sometimes. He let me thrive. He let me be me. And by giving me that creative freedom, he gave me the gift of growth.

Champion leaders have different personalities and quirks. While verbal recognition and appreciation always help, sometimes it's the subtle words that help us realize more of who we are. When receiving feedback, it's knowing the difference that counts.

Building Your Foundation of Emotional Intelligence

Dr. Peter Salovey, current president of Yale University, and Dr. John Mayer defined emotional intelligence as the ability to "recognize, understand, and manage our own emotions [and the ability to] recognize, understand, and influence the emotions of others. In practical terms, this means being aware that emotions can drive our behavior and impact people (positively and negatively), and learning how to manage those emotions—both our own and others'—especially when we are under pressure."[1]

Neuroscience research shows us that we react emotionally to a situation before we can think or respond logically. As a result, our ability to cultivate our emotional intelligence significantly affects how we "connect the CORD" (as I'll show you in Chapter 8). This means how we communicate, identify opportunities, build relationships, and make smart decisions. Throughout my career, I've found emotional intelligence is the greatest differentiating factor in achieving and sustaining long-term success and fulfillment.

Let's start with six key attributes of emotional intelligence that will help you build your leadership foundation. The best part is, you can learn and grow in these areas every day with focus and practice.

Self-Awareness

This chapter is all about *you*, which is where self-awareness begins. Self-awareness is the ability to understand and make sense of our emotions, and how we understand and know our character. Self-awareness matters immensely in leadership. Knowing our strengths, values, and beliefs helps us build a critical foundation of self-identity that guides us in everything we do. Self-awareness is also the art of "reading the room" and recognizing how others perceive us when we're connecting with them. We're always observing how others are taking us in. Last, self-awareness is significantly aided by feedback we receive from others. We cannot rely only on self-knowledge—we're enhanced and improved by the wisdom of others.

I discuss self-awareness in closer detail later in this chapter around building a game plan and delivering and receiving feedback.

An Understanding of Needs and Wants

Take a look at Abraham Maslow's hierarchy of needs (see Figure 2.1), and you'll see the physiological needs such as food, warmth, rest, and also safety and security. These must be met for us to function—to live. After we've met these basic life needs, we turn to professional needs such as salary, job function, autonomy, and level of impact that we want to create.

A want is something that is supplementary to our fundamental needs. It's often nice to have but not essential. Needs and wants vary greatly in leadership. You may need more team members to complete a project. Perhaps you want a flat organizational structure, or maybe you want more strategic thinkers on your team. Make sure you're able to clearly identify your needs and wants.

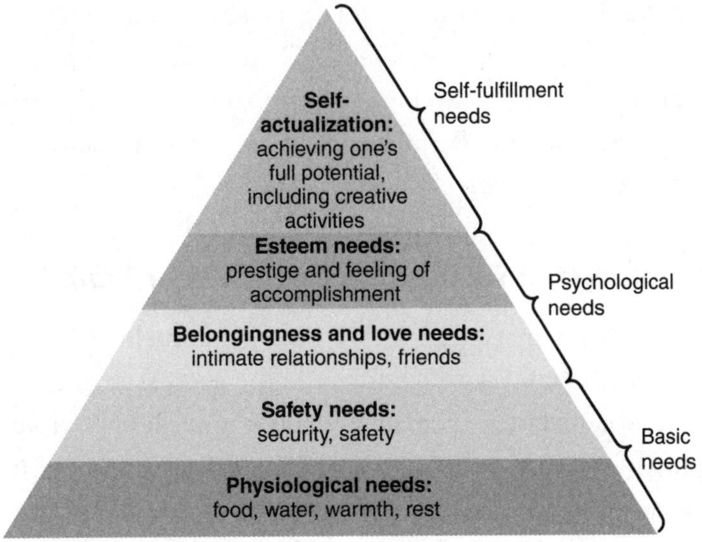

Figure 2.1 Abraham Maslow's hierarchy of needs.
Source: © John Wiley & Sons, Inc.

This provides you with perspective that guides your thinking and decision-making.

Empathy

As we discussed in Chapter 1, empathy is how we listen, care for, and lift others up through selfless leadership. Empathy is leadership from the heart that is other-seeking by nature. Empathy is a skill that can be learned through experiences. It's how you understand someone's needs and wants in an effort to help them learn and grow. The more empathetic you are in working with your team, the more engaged and driven to succeed your employees will be. They'll want to stick around and continue to form a bond to help your team become closer and more cohesive.

By being there for your team, showing curiosity and compassion, and getting involved to help when necessary, you're leading with "dirty hands." This leads to a feeling of shared ownership. Create open communication lines where people feel safer to explore, share, and generate ideas. Focus on how you want to treat others in the same way you'd want to be treated, and empathy will help you build connected relationships.

Championing the Success and Drive of Your Team

This is the quality that helps bridge emotional intelligence to championship leadership. Your investment in the success of your employees inspires camaraderie, creativity, and connection. I wrote about this value of altruism in *The Value of You*: "Altruism is the ultimate expression of selflessness. In other words, it's the opposite of egoism. Altruism is a **devotion** to the well-being of other people."[2]

When you're curious about your team members, they know it. When you're energized about helping them—they feel it. This team-first approach is a mindset that you can cultivate and focus on each day. Start thinking of what success looks like for your team. Listen to them! Ask them what it means to them on an individual and team level. Devoting yourself to your team's success is one of the virtues of championship leadership and requires putting the needs of others before your own.

Optimism

Optimistic leaders and teams create positive, forward-thinking organizations, ones that employees want to be a part of. Optimism is about having a positive long-term outlook and maintaining that vision through sunny skies and stormy seas. You want your long-term positive approach to rub off on your team members.

Optimism is not toxic positivity, which is inherently inauthentic and unrealistic. There will be tough days, and we can't be positive every second. But we can be optimistic, while acknowledging setbacks and defeats. This means maintaining steadfast belief, resilience, and positivity about the present and future. In a 2018 study published in the *Journal of Leadership & Organizational Studies*, Lisa C. Walsh and colleagues discovered a connection between positive leadership qualities, such as optimism, and the reduced probability of employees looking to leave their organization.[3]

Instilling a positive culture helps you to engage and retain your employees. Optimism is infectious. People want to be a part of an authentically positive culture. Think, plan, and look forward, and see the future with an opportunistic and optimistic outlook.

Adaptability

In simple terms, adaptability is knowing when to stay the course and knowing when it's time to change your direction. But adaptability is a lot more complex than that. To be adaptable as a leader, you're going to need to seamlessly shift from meetings with customers to meeting with team members to presenting before board members on your organization's strategic direction. You need to adapt to the constantly changing technological landscape and choose services and products that are right for the future of your business. You'll need to have a talent development and retention plan to ensure your employees want to stay for the long term.

The point is, business is always changing, which means you need to keep learning and remain open to change. The ability to adapt is influenced by two highly important skills: persistence and curiosity. Former CEO of Google, Eric Schmidt says: "Persistence is the single biggest predictor of future success. . . . And the second thing was curiosity. What do you care about? The combination of persistence and curiosity is a very good predictor of employee success. . . ."[4]

Become adaptable to how you build relationships and understand people, knowing how much emotions can influence the way we think and act.

Your Self-Awareness Game Plan

A tool that I've used with thousands of leaders is called the "Self-Awareness Game Plan." You can use the handy template in the "Leadership Resources" section to guide you. It's simple and straightforward and helps you understand the components of self-awareness. Here are each of the components:

- Passion;
- Values;
- Strengths;
- Purpose;
- Mission (Definition of Success);
- Success measures; and
- Goals (SMART).

Once you've established this foundation, you can perform a gap analysis of your skills. Begin with how you assess yourself to be currently and exactly what you want to gain in an effort to improve:

- Skills (current state); and
- Skills (future state).

Here is the key:

- **Passion:** The things that light the fire inside of you—which drive, motivate, and inspire you every time you think about them or do them.
- **Values:** A set of guiding principles and ideals that provide a standard for the way you behave and make decisions.

- **Strengths:** Your natural talents combined with the skills that you've acquired throughout your career. The things that you naturally do well.
- **Purpose:** Why you're doing what you're doing (the driving force or reasons behind setting your mission and goals).
- **Mission:** How you define success. If you're living and doing this, you will feel fulfilled, happy, and successful. You'll know that your actions have meaning.
- **Success measures:** Standards by which we determine whether our actions are living up to our mission (definition of success).
- **Goals:** Set "SMART" goals (the tangible results you desire to achieve). SMART stands for specific, measurable, achievable, relevant, and time-bound. George T. Doran first coined this term over 40 years ago. It's a clever mnemonic and easy-to-remember acronym that gives us a framework for goal setting.

This game plan may look easy, yet it's anything but simple. In fact, gaining clear self-awareness is very hard. Try one area at a time. And don't get too caught up in worrying about strictly professional or personal matters. Our personal and professional lives are inextricably linked. We show up to each with the experiences, emotions, and lessons learned from every part of our lives. You can interpret the game plan in a way that is right for you. There's no right or wrong. The main thing is to get started.

Completing this game plan will give you a self-awareness snapshot in time. Come back to it periodically, and as you go forward, start with a blank template. Gaining self-awareness helps us build self-confidence and belief in what we're doing. It gives us clarity of who we are. It prepares us for every interaction, decision, and opportunity.

As a supplement to the game plan, I highly recommend the CliftonStrengths assessment (formerly known as StrengthsFinder). It's a low-cost, high-value tool that will validate your understanding of your strengths and boost your confidence around that which you naturally do well.

> Questions for reflection:
>
> - Think about all of the roles that you play in life. Then ask yourself, "What do I need to feel affirmed in each of these roles?" (e.g. spouse, parent, son, leader, peer, just being *you*).
> - How often do you build in time throughout your day to affirm yourself and take breaks?
> - What are you currently doing to solicit feedback, and what could you improve?
> - What will bring you greater fulfillment in your current role?

Receiving Feedback and Maintaining Appointments with Yourself

Now that you've learned more about how to build your foundation of self-awareness, let's revisit another incredibly important part of self-awareness mentioned earlier: feedback. Feedback is a fundamental part of every great team and culture. Dr. Tasha Eurich tells us: "Leaders who focus on building both internal and external self-awareness, who seek honest feedback from loving critics, and who ask *what* instead of *why* can learn to see themselves more clearly—and reap the many rewards that increased self-knowledge delivers."[5]

You have control over how to deliver feedback and influence over how you receive it. I've developed my 5-Star Feedback Matrix to guide you through the basics of feedback. Pay close attention to the *focus* on each one in parentheses.

This matrix will guide you through ways you can ask for feedback and provide feedback to a variety of stakeholders. Here are some examples: your board, leadership team, steering committee, manager, peers, direct reports, frontline managers, and even customers.

Start here. Each item is focused on a group or person:

- Ask for feedback on how they feel operations overall are going. *(Focus on the business.)*
- Ask how they feel they're doing. *(Focus on their self-awareness.)*
- Ask for specific ways you can support them; for example, "I know you're working on the quarterly report; if I can answer any questions on x or y, please let me know." *(Focus on your management.)*
- Provide feedback on what they're doing well and how they can improve. *(Focus on their growth.)*
- Ask how they feel you're doing. *(Focus on your growth through their eyes.)*

Always ask for candor and provide it. Let each stakeholder know you're looking for the unfiltered truth because it will help everyone grow. If you're looking to be placated, feedback will be a waste of your time. If you're seeking only external validation, this won't be as helpful. I encourage leaders to focus on valuable input that helps them improve for the present and future.

From there, you're able to lock in an appointment with yourself at least once per month. Regardless of whether you have a great support structure, which may include an executive coach, or a close inner circle, you'll find tremendous value in processing your thoughts by carving out a 15–30-minute self-appointment. Determine how you can take the feedback you've received, and make it actionable. Analyze the positives and negatives, and foremost, determine what you can act on. It's about "locking in the gains" of new knowledge, to use a weightlifting analogy. Understand what you need to improve. Then, start doing it with consistency. Build to the next progression—set the next goal for yourself.

Revisit the game plan to assess degree of difficulty. Ask yourself: Is this an area of strength to improve or more of a growth opportunity? Similarly, discover how this is in alignment with your purpose, mission, and goals. Building in this time each month provides accountability and allows you to utilize your self-awareness to reflect—a topic we'll focus on more in Chapter 5.

Managing Energy, Outlets, and Burnout

As we started to see once the effects of the COVID pandemic began to settle in, burnout became a very real issue for many individuals—and organizations. Burnout has affected millions of employees, and often affects women more than men. A 2022 Women in the Workplace study from Lean In and McKinsey showed "43% of women leaders are burned out, compared to only 31% of men at their level."[6] An overwhelming workload, fast pace, lack of breaks, time pressures, and a lack of social support are classic causes of burnout. Many of these were exacerbated as we began to move further away from having connected relationships.

Burnout is something that can take over before we can even recognize it, which raises the question, What are some classic symptoms of burnout?

- Stress;
- An inability to think clearly;

- Feeling easily agitated;
- Withdrawal or lack of motivation/interest;
- Feeling overwhelmed;
- Cynicism;
- Feeling tired and energy depleted;
- Poor memory; and
- Negative mindset.

It's critical to acknowledge that burnout is real and to have frequent check-ins with your team to support their mental, emotional, and social well-being. Encourage team members to utilize vacation days, and reevaluate each team member's workload to make sure everyone is appropriately staffed.

Dr. Pamela Coburn-Litvak, a neuroscientist and stress researcher, focuses on resilience as a psychological tool to help manage burnout. She told me the key is to be aware of the signs of burnout in the first place. By understanding causes, we're better equipped to target the sources of stress-induced burnout and manage it effectively. It's all about determining what we have control over, what we don't, and how we leverage tools to effectively manage stress when we experience it.

She said, "The feeling that we need to get ahead necessitates that we have to be working as hard as we can for as long as we can. What we really want to do is replace that mistaken belief with a stress-reducing belief that will increase our productivity and mitigate burnout. For example, if I prioritize taking vacations and breaks, this will allow me to recharge my battery. It's imperative that we focus on cultivating a positive mindset."[7]

I encourage my clients to focus on their energy and outlets. Sources of energy can be exercise, time in solitude, connection time, brainstorming, or simply coffee time. We want to find time in our schedules for the things that energize us. In the same way, we should recognize what enervates us—the things that rob us of our positivity and energy.

Likewise, it's critical to know our outlets—all the ways to relieve stress. This can include going for a walk, taking a break, or practicing mindfulness.

Affirmations, Mindfulness, and Visualization

A commitment to personal development doesn't have to be time-consuming, nor mentally exhausting. Quite the opposite. You can invest time each day for self-care and reap maximum benefits. Begin with positive affirmations.

Affirm yourself and speak positively about what you've done, what you're doing, and what you plan to do. You can do this in writing, say them to yourself quietly, or speak them out. Be kind to yourself, and focus on the positives. This has a calming effect on our mind and body, and it helps us replace negative thoughts or stress with positive, nurturing thoughts.

Practice mindfulness to be fully present, to bring conscious awareness to your thoughts, and to improve your self-awareness. It's so important to free ourselves from worry about the future or regret of the past. Mindfulness helps us become better leaders. I encourage you to see it as a soft skill. It helps improve our listening and our responses in each situation.

Yenushka Karunaratne, a mindfulness educator, talks about the importance of creating the space for our thoughts. "Mindfulness allows us to step back—to become aware—and then ask questions like, 'How am I managing myself?' and 'What story am I telling myself?'"[8] It can create a space between our initial thoughts and our feelings and actions that follow. When we're able to take a step back, we're able to make smarter decisions.

She further adds, "If we're constantly in fight/flight mode, we will continue to struggle. Mindfulness helps us to better manage our thoughts and emotions without escaping or trying to fight against them. By practicing mindfulness, we become more aware and accepting of our emotions."

Visualization is a practice developed in the sports world that can have direct application to the way we lead ourselves and others. Dedicate time and use your creative imagination to visually see yourself in a process. See yourself in a team meeting recognizing one of your colleagues and presenting them with an award. Visualize yourself sharing the news of winning a new deal. See yourself achieving a meaningful goal that makes you feel fulfilled. Visualize yourself thriving and achieving your goals. I've found champion leaders have a knack of visualizing themselves achieving success before they do it.

Sometimes it can feel lonely as a leader. You have a lot of responsibility. Caring for others takes a lot of effort and energy. Remember to recharge your battery. These three tools will help you to build confidence, fortitude, and belief.

The Power of Belief

"I believe in believe!"

—Ted Lasso

Oh yeah, I'm thinking *this* is the season AFC Richmond finally reaches the pinnacle of English football.

If you know, you know. By that I mean, you might be familiar with the Apple TV+ show *Ted Lasso*, which captured the hearts and minds of millions over the last several years. If you're not, it's a story only Hollywood could concoct. The show centers on an American football coach—turned English *football* manager—who's improbably asked, by the team's new owner, to lead fictional English football club, AFC Richmond. The Greyhounds are one of the 20 teams competing in the English Premier League, the top flight of English football. It's crazy and goofy, and yet it tugs at our heart strings.

The character of Ted Lasso, played by Jason Sudeikis, is as authentic and sweet as a heaping plate of Kansas City–style barbecue. He's kind, curious, empathetic, and trustworthy. With his Midwestern twang, sunny optimism, and homespun metaphors, he doesn't quite fit in—at first—in London. But over time, he begins to win the hearts and minds of his team—and we, the viewers. His team spirit is inspired by extraordinary belief. He devoutly believes in himself, his team—and in every person in the organization. Deep down, we wish we had someone who championed us the way Ted Lasso does AFC Richmond.

The genius of the show is that Ted Lasso gets us to believe even more in ourselves—and in how we can positively influence the people in our lives. It takes action, to be sure, but it all begins with belief.

When it comes to TV entertainment options, there's lot of doom and gloom out there and, well, darkness. *Ted Lasso* brings us light. It shows us just how important culture is to a team—and to an organization. Ted Lasso challenges, disarms, and charms, winning everyone over with an unconventional approach. Jason Sudeikis's title character inspires others through his own quirky brand of authenticity, assertiveness, candor, and empathy (see Chapter 1). But it's his ability to get us to "believe" that transcends television comedy, allowing us to find that belief in ourselves.

Believe in yourself. Believe in others. Believe that things will work out in your favor, despite the myriad challenges that stand in your way.

Throughout my career of coaching leaders, every time I've gotten to the core of what has made the true leadership difference in their careers, it goes along the lines of "_______ believed in me."

Someone lifted that person up. Someone championed their career at some point. An organization took a chance on them. That *chance* was the spark they needed to grow and prosper. It started with words of encouragement that led to action. Building relationships isn't always easy. It takes effort, authenticity, and belief in someone else. Take it from Ted Lasso, we could use a little more of his brand of leadership.

Do you believe?

Inspiring Belief

An article from *MIT Sloan Management Review* shows that relationships in leadership are rooted in credibility, which comes down to two things: "perceived competence (people's faith in the leader's knowledge, skills, and ability to do the job) and trustworthiness (their belief in his or her values and dependability)."[9]

In business, things are going to change. We certainly saw that over the past four years during the COVID pandemic. It's why a championship culture is even more important today. Belief is not just a part of your culture; it's the underlying core value that you can give to every person in your organization. It will help provide stability as things change around you.

When you believe in what you do, you're more likely to help others see the intrinsic value of their work and the valuable contributions they make to the team. It's why I like to tell clients: "Make *your* passion *their* passion. Let *your* belief inspire *their* belief. And in return, make *their* passion and belief *yours*."

That is the essence of inspirational leadership.

Aspire to make a difference. Do what is right, fair, and just. Ensure that your actions are aligned with your values. Speak up when something isn't right. Encourage your team! That is belief—and it makes you a powerful proclaimer of the truth. We can be champions of our culture and create this *Champions League,* where we lead and inspire others to see the best in themselves. In turn, they'll want to champion people throughout your organization by unifying your message.

Be a champion who listens and prioritizes the value of each interaction. This has a ripple effect on culture, innovation, and bottom-line results. Believe in what's possible by getting back to your roots and remembering why you do what you do. This *Champions League* is for the leaders who genuinely want to lift others up and support their employees for life.

I'm seeing each day just how much transactional, impersonal leadership is turning people away and out the door for better opportunities. Personalized, authentic connection matters. When you inspire belief in your employees, you bring people closer together. This creates a culture that employees want to be a part of. It helps customers see the "heart of a champion." Customers want to work with organizations who solve their problems, but they also want a partner who listens to them and believes in what they're doing.

Championing Your Growth with Self-Confidence and Self-Advocacy

How do we develop self-confidence?

It's a question I've asked the brightest business leaders in the world, and it's one I'm asked by audiences all the time. I believe it boils down to three things: preparation, mindset, and experience.

Hard stop!

Now, ask yourself, "How have I grown in confidence throughout my career—and life?"

As I look at my own, I've grown in confidence as a child, student, athlete, businessman, writer, and person because of each experience. I've learned from each experience, figured out what to take with me going forward, and then prepared my mind for the next opportunity. While accomplishments go a long way toward growing our confidence, we learn even more through adversity—if we're willing to stay positive. Confidence is a state of mind. It's part of our attitude. It's empowered by belief, yes, and it's strengthened by *doing*, and reaping the lessons learned and rewards that come from taking action.

Famed psychologist Albert Bandura wrote about self-efficacy, which gives us wisdom to help us apply confidence to what we do.[10] Self-efficacy applies to the belief we can succeed in specific situations, while confidence applies more to our belief in our abilities. The two are related. Bandura's self-efficacy theory focuses on how our behaviors can be influenced by the perceptions we have about our competence. Higher self-efficacy means that we often perform better and increase in motivation and self-confidence.

Bandura defined self-efficacy as "people's judgments of their capabilities to organize and execute courses of action required to attain designated types of performances."[11]

Here are Bandura's four sources of self-efficacy that significantly affect our self-confidence:[12]

1. Mastery experiences (performances);
2. Vicarious experiences (observing others);
3. Verbal persuasion (words of encouragement); and
4. Physiological and emotional states (our feelings).

The power of *doing*, combined with observing, receiving encouragement, and managing our emotions, affects the development of our confidence. How we prepare and how we see ourselves (mindset) after each experience builds belief and self-confidence in our abilities. It creates momentum, driving us to perform at our best for every new opportunity that comes our way.

As we think about our mindset, I ask you to think about the times you've persevered and overcome obstacles. Chances are, you've adapted, become more resilient, and sharpened your focus to learn from each experience. Neuroscientist and chief research officer at New York University Dr. Stacie Bloom writes in the *Wall Street Journal*:

> To be self-confident—and to bolster confidence in others—we should deliberately shut down our inner critic, over and over again. At the cellular level, this requires building new connections. . .We can build new connections and change our thoughts and behavior by being brave and overcoming obstacles. . .(and) by learning something new—whether that's a card game or a data analytics platform—and committing that knowledge to memory through repetition or practice. . .(and) by shifting our usual routines and reactions.[13]

Growing in self-confidence takes time. One of the biggest misconceptions I've found is the thought that our education ends in the school system—whether high school, college, graduate school, or beyond. The greatest driver of your leadership education is you. Your leadership education is lifelong! Champion leaders continue to practice the fundamentals and learn throughout their careers. Realizing your options and building in this self-education component will be vital to your long-term success.

Even the world's most successful leaders have mentors and coaches—people who champion their growth and help them see things from a new perspective. But remember this: the onus to grow and elevate yourself to where you want to go comes back to you.

As discussed in Chapter 1, part of that is self-advocacy. Self-advocacy looks like this:

- Developing a mindset of courage and confidence to influence stakeholders to understand your ideas and how you plan to innovate;
- Creating a vision for your career that has depth—a long-term plan for what you want to do and why you want to do it; and
- Influencing others to show how your organization will benefit by you taking on a more prominent leadership role.

Self-advocacy is a long-term game. Dedicate time each week to acknowledge the successes you've experienced as an individual and with your team.

Successes and failures will come and go throughout your life. It's what you take forward from all of your experiences that will develop your confidence. To support that point, Stanford University management professor Dr. Robert I. Sutton writes in *Harvard Business Review*:

> After people succeed at something, it is especially important to have them focus on what things went wrong. They learn more than if they just focus on success (so, don't just gloat and congratulate yourself about what you did right; focus on what could go even better next time). When failure happens, the most important thing is to have an after event review to provoke sufficiently deep thinking—whether you talk about successes or failures is less important.[14]

To develop confidence, stay positive and perseverant. Profit by finding the lessons in each of your experiences. Never look back with regret. Look forward.

Solidifying Your Structure

We started this chapter with recognizing and establishing your foundation, and we close it with solidifying your structure over time. Your authenticity and identity define who you are as a leader—that's truly your character. Your leadership foundation evolves over time through a lifelong education of leadership learning and growth. This is best born from experience; try new things, see what sticks and what doesn't. It's also the work you do for yourself, reevaluating your foundation to always make sure it's firm and knowing what to add on and what to subtract. Remain open-minded to new thoughts, ideas, and perspectives.

Coach John Wooden said, "It's what you learn after you know it all that counts." So remember: stay humble and aware of the many ways you can learn and gather new information. This can come from:

- One-on-one or team meetings;
- Reading books, taking courses, and attending conferences;
- Reviewing successes and failures;
- Revisiting past lessons learned from earlier jobs in your career;
- Getting feedback from trusted sources; and
- Executive coaching.

The goal is not overanalysis or over-reflection; too much can be destructive. So put a time limit on things. Take time each week to revisit a particular area of growth, and stick to your time limit. Here's how you can do it. Ask yourself:

- What worked well?
- What didn't?
- What made the difference in having a positive or successful experience? and
- What did I learn? What can I discard? What can I take with me?

Categorize your learnings through areas such as people management, business outcomes, and innovation. In Chapter 3 we'll focus on discovering the motivating factors and purpose that serve as the motivational fuel that drives you forward to champion others.

You Exercise

Put together your game plan. Once you've done so, think deeper on how you can model these behaviors each day for yourself and the people you lead. If you're willing, review this with your board chair, manager, a mentor, or executive coach to get feedback. Go further—become more conscientious at building time into your day for "energy and outlets." It's great to have a foundation. It's even more important to evolve and find ways to sustain your growth as you navigate through each situation.

Champion's Checklist (Tools and Takeaways)

- ☑ Build time into each day, even 15 minutes, for self-care.
- ☑ Prioritize receiving feedback from a variety of sources on a regular basis.
- ☑ Ask yourself, "What did I learn today that made me better?"
- ☑ Advocate for yourself. Proudly speak to your accomplishments and how they've helped the organization.
- ☑ Recognize what you need and what you want. You'll know the difference.

Chapter 3

Why (*Discover the Purpose and Motivating Factors That Drive High-Performing Teams*)

"As a leader, I feel my job is to set the vision and the goals for the company, and then to work with everyone to empower them to dream big and crazy. I want to set them up to do the best work of their lives and to achieve those crazy, big goals."

—Melanie Perkins

The man we know today as "Coach K" wasn't exactly a legend in the early spring of 1980. Before the national championships, 1,200+ wins, bestselling books, countless All-American players, and icon status as a champion leader, Mike Krzyzewski was at the start of a long journey. He was trying to guide Duke University's men's basketball team to a winning season.

Coach K's first three years in Durham, North Carolina, were up and down, but there was more down than up. Toward the end of his third season at the helm (Duke's second consecutive losing season), things weren't looking good. And they were about to get worse.

Duke faced Virginia in the quarterfinals of the 1983 ACC Tournament. They were outplayed, outcoached, and embarrassed. Virginia annihilated the Blue Devils, 109-66. It was a crushing end to the season—one that didn't provide optimism heading into a long off season. And for Coach K, the future was uncertain. Rumors swirled, creating speculation that he could be fired only three seasons after taking the job.

Following the loss at The Omni in Atlanta, a group of Duke basketball staffers went out to dinner at a nearby Denny's. The men ate and chatted; it was a somber scene. They wondered, What just hit us? Duke's sports information director tried to look at things in a positive light. As the staff ate their meals, he raised his glass of iced tea, looked around the table, and said, "Here's to forgetting about tonight. . . ."

Before he could finish, Coach K stopped him.

There was a pause of dead silence. Several seconds went by.

As Coach K would later recall, what happened next was "probably the most important moment" of his career.[1]

Krzyzewski asked the man to put his glass down. He reached over and picked up his glass of water, looked around the table, and said, "Here's to never forgetting about tonight." (For more information, see *ESPN Films Presents: The Class That Saved Coach K.*)

The message was clear. Duke's men's basketball program would begin to build its present and future on the foundation of its lowest point. Coach K made sure no one would ever forget where they came from nor the terrible feeling from that lopsided defeat. He knew the importance lay in making sense of why it happened, and how those lessons could help them move forward. That loss catalyzed Coach K and his staff, as well as the new, talented players coming to Duke. They used it as motivation that energized and propelled them to unprecedented heights.

Only three years later, Duke played in the national championship game. Eight years later, they won their first of back-to-back national championships.

Sometimes, our greatest losses serve as the most powerful moments of our lives. Reframing the way we see defeat and adversity allows us to learn our greatest lessons. It clarifies our purpose and motivation to do what we know we can achieve. Now, over 40 years later, Coach K is regarded as one of the greatest coaches in American sports history. Duke men's basketball is as synonymous with winning as any program in the country.

One thread I've found in working with thousands of global business leaders is how many of them have clearly defined motivational drivers. Even more, somewhere along the way, there was a moment of reckoning that served as a seminal moment in their careers—and in their lives. A catalyzing force that became a signature part of their why for the work they do.

For some, purpose is "in the blood" and it's been part of them for years. Yet there are always significant moments for every leader where a line is drawn. For Coach K, it was March 11, 1983—the night he and Duke men's basketball would never forget. For others, it's "I'll never, ever go back to *that*" or "I will find a way" for a cause, a business, or a group of people.

Champion leaders' *why* and *who* are inextricably linked and intertwined. Both serve as the driving force for why they do what they do. They're motivated by serving people. When what you want for yourself is the opportunity to bring out the best in others, you'll discover what it truly means to lead.

Motivating Factors (for You and Your Employees)

When you see the word "motivation," what's the first thing you think of?

Motivation is the spark—the driving force—that empowers our mindset and strengthens our preparation and commitment to achieve our goals. *Motivation* is one of those words that people often misinterpret because it has a lot of meaning. We can motivate ourselves (self-motivation), we can be motivated (and influenced) by others, and we can motivate others. Motivation is real. You know this because of the strides you've made in your own career. Something or someone was encouraging and driving you to be better. Maybe you've been able to find what makes someone else tick and impel them to do their best work.

So what is your driving force? What are you most passionate about?

As leaders, it's essential to be crystal clear on what this motivation is for ourselves, the people we lead, and our organization.

Whether you're looking to formulate a strategy, drive business results, or shape culture, it's best to try and align as much as you can with your team members' motivating factors. Everything won't always fit seamlessly. But the more motivated people are to show up, the more engaged they will be. They'll be more likely to contribute and want to stay at your organization. I ask you to think about the factors that help to build your intrinsic motivation and similarly, how your leadership style helps lift others up to do great things. That's how you motivate others.

Motivation is not about continuously driving people to do things that aren't in their best interest. It's demotivating as an employee when you feel you're not recognized, rewarded, or appreciated for your hard work. This is where some organizations and leaders get motivation wrong—or worse yet, think it doesn't work. Empathizing with your team, in both group and one-on-one settings, allows you to better understand each person's needs and wants—and motivating factors.

To build connection, start going *deeper* in conversation. Find what your team members are passionate about. Personalize the conversation and ask open-ended questions to get to know someone. Remember where you came from; be curious and emotionalize your stories.

In my work with leaders, I find a strong linkage between motivation and spirituality. Namely, in the core values that center us, the purpose that powers us, and the belief that our team comes before any individual. It's why your leadership foundation matters to what motivates you and others.

The Herzberg motivation theory, also known as the two-factor theory or motivation-hygiene theory, came from the work of renowned psychologist Frederick Herzberg during the 1950s. It breaks down factors that influence both job satisfaction and dissatisfaction.

Let's look first at examples of motivators that arise from intrinsic conditions and provide positive feelings and satisfaction:

- Recognition or appreciation;
- The work itself;
- Upward mobility;
- Autonomy and responsibility; and
- Overall job satisfaction and role happiness.

Now, here are hygiene factors that arise from extrinsic conditions and incentivize us to do our jobs. They don't directly motivate us, but without them we experience dissatisfaction:

- Pay;
- Title;
- Job security;
- Work from home/virtual;
- Fringe benefits, time off; and
- Company policies.

According to the two-factor theory, job satisfaction and dissatisfaction are not opposing forces; instead, they exist independently. It comes down to how we address these factors. It's your job, as a leader, to be mindful of these factors and to have regular check-ins to ensure they're being met. Keep reading to find out how to do so.

Building Connections with Individualization

One of the top strengths I highlight for champion leaders is *individualization*, which also profiles as one of the CliftonStrengths. They define those who use this strength as people who "are intrigued with the unique qualities of each person. They have a gift for figuring out how different people can work together productively."[2] Every person has unique qualities and motivations (or motivating factors) for why they show up each day. Think of this as their why. Knowing from Chapter 2 how powerful your own why is, you're aware of how brightly this burns for others.

We build meaningful relationships by understanding where someone is coming from, what they care about, and why it matters to them. That's why conversations that focus on your employees' motivating factors lead to connection. By doing this, you break down the initial fear and apprehension that comes with getting to know someone. And let me clear something up here as well: champion leaders aren't *only* extroverts. In fact, extroverts can struggle with small talk and trying to understand someone's personal interests and desires. This ability to connect doesn't come naturally to most people, so don't get discouraged if this doesn't come naturally to you. You have to start somewhere. Make a joke—heck, make a bad joke! Have fun. Think of all the benefits that come from having a closer relationship with someone and let that be your North Star when building connection.

Some of the best champion leaders in the world, such as Microsoft CEO Satya Nadella, are introverts. Yet they prioritize empathy and emotionality and build powerful relationships. They thrive on deep relationships where they get to know someone and build trust. This creates energy and emotion, serving as a catalyzing force.

In an interview Nadella said, "There is no simple thing that is always under your control, so the idea is that you have got to create energy all around you."[3]

Individualization requires us to go *deep* and invest time in understanding what makes someone tick. Individualization is about tailoring the way we communicate to meet someone where they are. Meaning, we won't communicate with each person exactly the same way. We need to work to understand someone's needs and wants and what interests them. We adapt, learn, and put ourselves in a better position to help them by asking open-ended, concise questions.

Individualizing the way we communicate isn't just talking for the sake of talking. It should *never* be viewed as unnecessary time. Think about it: What is it like when you don't have a relationship with someone? It's hard to influence or help someone until we get to know them. I encourage you to be a detective and get to know your team members and colleagues. Let people know they're highly valued. Do it without judgment, without assuming, and without attempting to solve their problems. The highest compliment you can pay an excellent listener is to thank them for giving you their undivided attention. If you feel listened to, acknowledged, and valued, you're going to feel a closer bond with that person. This works both ways.

I've found that champion leaders have a burning fire inside of them that drives them to make everyone around them better. There's a psychological commitment to make a difference in people's lives. It's guided by fairness and vision that bridges influencing and strategic thinking with relationship building and execution.

Connected relationships lead to exchanging ideas and bringing people together to achieve a mission. This inspires innovation, optimism, and collective grit that can ignite the spirit of an entire organization.

Having top-down organizational leadership over someone guarantees very little. If you don't work on your relationships each day, you run the risk of losing them. Start by asking each person what their passions and hobbies are. Ask them about their family. Ask about their professional ambitions. Build this time into meeting agendas! This is how you begin to individualize your approach to grow each relationship.

Questions for reflection:

- How can you develop consistency around building relationships with your team?
- What techniques do you find yourself using to motivate others?
- What are you most passionate about?
- How well do you manage change—both personally and professionally?

The Science Behind Emotional Intelligence

Neuroscience is the scientific study of the nervous system and how it functions. It provides us with unique insights on how to lead with emotional intelligence. Starting with the components of self-awareness (the way we recognize and manage emotions), neuroscience can help us improve how we process emotions and use logic and reason. It's helpful to learn about the parts of the brain that matter in building our EQ.

Let's start with the limbic brain. The limbic brain is involved in our emotional and behavioral responses. It provides responses to the wide range of emotions we face daily. For example, this could be our instinct to react with tough words for someone we disagree with in a meeting or to stand up for a colleague we feel has been treated unfairly.

Within the limbic brain, the amygdala serves as the control station for our fight-or-flight response. It guides our emotional recognition and management and is responsible for our memory formation. Our amygdala processes emotions such as fear, doubt, anger, gratitude, and happiness, influencing every thought and decision. As we become more self-aware, we gain deeper insights into the ebb and flow of these emotional currents and their role in shaping our choices.

The frontal lobe is known as our thinking brain for decision-making, logic, and problem solving. It gives us the gift of introspection, allowing us to reflect on our emotions. The frontal lobe equips us with effective communication tools such as maintaining steady eye contact and using clear language. As we learned, our emotional responses precede our logical thinking. Maintaining awareness of this will help us in every interaction.

Dr. Michael L. Platt, psychology professor at the University of Pennsylvania, says, "We know from neuroscience, for example, that if we want to communicate more effectively with the people we manage, then we need to be simple, clear and concise—and make eye contact as much as possible. The neuroscience is very strong on this, and those kinds of practices will lead to better chemistry with the person you're communicating with . . ."[4]

Sharing space within the limbic system, the basal ganglia is responsible for our learning, habits, cognition, and emotional responses. To master our behaviors means creating excellent habits and improving our emotional intelligence. Multitasking, while very appealing, leads to errors. Don't believe me? Take this from the Cleveland Clinic: "We're really wired to be monotaskers. . . . One study found that just 2.5 percent of people are able to multitask effectively. For the rest of us, our attempts to do multiple activities at once aren't actually that . . . we become less efficient and more likely to make a mistake."[5]

It's best to focus with total concentration on what you're doing in that moment. Even in its restful state, our brain demands a substantial 20%–25% of our energy. By managing and reducing fear-induced reactions such as stress and anxiety, we allow our brain to function at its optimal capacity.

The study of the brain shows the transformative power of "putting ourselves in someone else's shoes" by actively listening and allowing someone the freedom to solve problems. This approach ignites creativity, drives innovation, and fosters smart habits. It shows us that leading with empathy is how we drive powerful connection.

We gain new knowledge on the human brain each day. For your leadership, it helps to gain a greater understanding of your emotions and to know how they create memorable leadership experiences for your team.

Altruism, Connection, and Commitment

When we see our desire to help others as part of our purpose, the more likely we'll be to take action. Our passion is tied to our purpose and motivates us to help others. Writing in *Time* magazine, author Jenny Santi says, "Our passion should be the foundation for our giving. It is not how much we give, but how much love we put into giving."[6]

It's why altruism matters so much and why guiding others and lifting others up comes from putting the needs of people at the top of our priority list. It also comes from being connected. UCLA psychology professor Matthew Lieberman discusses this in his book *Social: Why Our Brains Are Wired to Connect*. He said, "Being socially connected is our brain's lifelong passion. It's been baked into our operating system for tens of millions of years."[7]

This pertains to helping others and to sharing ideas. Lieberman said: "We're wired to see things and think, 'How can I use this to help other people that I know?' I can have the most brilliant idea for an invention, but if I can't convey that to other people in a way that they'll help me build it and market it to other people, it's just an idea in my head. If we're not socially connected, even great ideas wither."

Connection is formed when everyone has a feeling of ownership—that they're contributing to a successful team effort. If people are in silos and not speaking to one another, then it's critical to address this right away. Increase the frequency with which you're communicating

Resilience

One of the most important things I look for in healthy, thriving organizations is how resilient they are—and how well they manage change. Let's first define what resilience is: resilience determines our ability to bounce back, recover, and move forward from challenges and adversity. In leadership, this pertains to:

- Poor performance;
- Relationship conflict;
- Low employee morale;
- Unmotivated or disengaged teams;
- Losing business; and
- Not meeting sales/revenue goals.

The secret of resilience is about how we see opportunities in front of us. The more we accept that there will be adversity and challenges, the more we begin to see these otherwise difficult moments as opportunities, not negatives. Thinking negatively elicits negative emotions such as fear, stress, or worry. And we know that we're not performing at our best when we're worried or afraid of what comes next.

After any setback or failure, it's critical that we evaluate the experience and determine *why* and *how* it happened, and most importantly, *what* we can do about it. We need to tweak, make adjustments, and learn from what we just did. Make an "acceptance appointment" with yourself. Admit what went wrong. Come to peace with it, take a deep breath, and move forward.

It's not time to beat ourselves up or criticize ourselves harshly. It's about using emotional intelligence to build resilience in the face of adversity. This means preparing ourselves with confidence, managing our emotions, and developing a plan to succeed. We all need to get smarter, wiser, and more adaptable to advance forward in our careers. You do this by learning how to use adversity to your advantage.

Professor Nancy Koehn of Harvard Business School says, "Resilience is . . . not a DNA deposit that was made when we were born. . . . It's a learned capability and it's very much like a muscle in that we make it stronger by using it. . . . Each time we navigate through a crisis and find a little strength in it, we can pick out an insight we can learn from and resolve not to get bitter, weaker, smaller, or more frightened, but, rather, to get the tiniest bit braver."[8]

There's no surprise that qualities such as optimism, courage, perseverance—and yes, humor—matter when it comes to being resilient. High-performing teams are built by *people*. We're all human, and we all have emotions to share. That's what makes teams who have big hearts, and who lead with resilience, truly great. Overcoming challenges helps us to become mentally and emotionally stronger—and more resilient. It further strengthens our individual and team purpose.

Dr. Karen Whitfield and Dr. Kyle Wilby write: "Articulating why people do the work they do is essential in order to understand purpose, and is thought to be directly related to resilience development. . . . There is evidence to suggest that individuals who have a clear purpose have lower stress levels and a higher degree of resilience."[9]

Connect your leadership purpose to having a resilient mindset and instill this with your team. When your team adopts the belief that every adversity is an opportunity to get better, you will always persevere through change—and every challenge that comes your way.

A Note on Big Picture versus Tactical Details

What I've found separates successful leaders from the pack is their ability to see—and navigate between—the big picture and smaller details. In other words, to adapt and see things strategically and tactically. As a leader, it's always best to maintain a strategic, higher-level view, but at times you'll need to get into the details to help make a decision or identify an issue.

As a general rule of thumb, adopt the 80/20 rule for time balance. You want to spend about 80% of your time on the big picture, highest impact strategic items that improve productivity. Here's where to begin:

- Articulate the organizational vision and strategic goals on a frequent basis. Keep your team's eyes on the prize.
- You cannot do it all. Accept what you can and cannot do, and don't get too bogged down by the tactical details.
- Set clear boundaries and reevaluate these each week.
- Define who owns each key function. Trust your team members to own particular business functions, and be the subject matter expert on those.
- Delegate! Stay informed at a strategic level on how things are going.
- Ask questions that tie back to strategic goals. Those questions should tie back to the why and also to your mission and goals.

Inspiring Change

Every successful change effort is spearheaded by excellent communications. I encourage you to focus on quality and frequency, as well as inclusivity, so you are well prepared. Critical change actions you can take include the following:

- First, before you can drive a successful change initiative, you need to understand and clearly explain the *why* to your stakeholders. This ensures clarity, conciseness, and control in communicating your vision.

- Develop a well-structured communications plan, outlining your objectives, reasons for pursuing them, and the organizational benefits. Always keep in mind that even when you believe you're communicating sufficiently, it's likely you need to communicate even more.
- Identify the champions throughout your organization and form a diverse coalition of people who will support and propel the initiative. That's why investing time and effort in nurturing relationships is crucial. Change is made possible by people who are willing to support your vision and communicate with you in urgent and important times.
- Demonstrate decisiveness and uphold your commitments. Do what you say you're going to do—follow through. Implement your vision and communications plan while remaining adaptable to handle disruptions. Don't give in to fear or excessive analysis; instead, trust in your well-thought-out plan.
- Engage actively and empower others, providing transparent and honest responses to their inquiries. Embrace your employees' feedback and proactively seek ways to involve them in the change effort, making them an integral part of the process.
- Ensure consistent messaging from your peers and colleagues to all employees. Keep your communications clear and straightforward, both in writing and speech, to foster understanding. Strive for alignment on every decision made within the organization.
- Be an optimistic realist. Have a positive outlook, but always provide an honest assessment of how things are going.

Focus on the high-impact changes that you want to influence. It's always best to begin first with an ideal state, not yet factoring in risks. I also like to say, don't "pressure test" for time just yet. And don't be concerned about resistance. Start with what *could* be possible, and then work to mitigate and manage risks. Don't immediately rule things out without trying first. Every great change effort and innovation first encounters some level of skepticism or resistance. That's a given! Worrying early on about "what could be?" will slow down your strategy and the ideas that come with it.

Some changes are initiated by circumstances and by nature are reactive. But what about proactive changes, ones where you want to innovate and create opportunities that aren't there today? Your first objective might be to raise awareness and help the organization see it as a need. There's an educational element to every successful change initiative that is backed by a clear vision. Change needs to be understood in both the present and future for how it will affect finances, resources, work prioritization, and of course, people. Start here, and focus on what you want to drive and how to effectively communicate this to everyone involved.

The Next One

When legendary NFL quarterback Tom Brady played college football at the University of Michigan, he formed a friendship with the school's longtime equipment manager, Jon Falk. That man had seen it all. For over four decades, Falk was there for the good and the bad. Mostly, lots of wins. One national championship. Many conference championship teams, with accompanying championship rings.

Jon Falk knew a winner when he saw one.

Several years ago, Brady returned to campus and found his way to the football locker room. As he toured the facility, he began to dream. He gazed up at the many championship banners from over the years and smiled as he saw Falk. Brady turned to him and asked him which championship was his favorite.

Falk approached him and said, "You know what, Tom? You know what my favorite ring is? The next one."[10]

Celebrate and embrace every challenge, change, and adversity that comes your way. That alone builds resilience for you and your team. But always have the motivation and desire to forge ahead toward the next opportunity. That's what I encourage you to think about.

The next one.

Why Exercise

Start by describing three things that are most important to you professionally and three things that are most important to you personally. Then, go around to each person and ask them to describe theirs. What patterns are you seeing? How are these insights bringing you closer to each team member?

Professional examples could be the work itself, the benefits received from their work, or opportunities for advancement.

Personal examples could be family, personal growth, or learning. The goal is to increase your team members' awareness of each other's motivational drivers and to create synergies to help support these.

Champion's Checklist (Tools and Takeaways)

☑ Make the effort to understand the top motivational drivers for each person on your team.

☑ Remember to think about why you're doing what you're doing and how this aligns with your values.

☑ Recognize relationship-building time as one of the most important drivers of team success.

☑ Have the self-awareness to find opportunity in every challenge you face.

☑ Use the "ABC's" of communication to guide your change efforts: accuracy, brevity, and clarity.

Chapter 4

Your Organization (*Use Empathy and Social Skills to Make Everyone around You Better*)

"At the end of the day, the success of every company is about its people."

—Mary Barra

Life's best leadership lessons are taught at home. For General Motors (GM) chair and CEO Mary Barra, her leadership education started at the kitchen table.

Barra grew up in a close-knit family in Michigan. When it was dinnertime at the Barra household, everyone would gather around to talk, listen, and share stories. "Everyone" meant family, friends, and relatives. If they'd stopped by after lunch or work, they were there to stay for dinner. Barra's mother wouldn't turn any family or friends away. Everyone was included. There was always room for one more. This inclusive approach rubbed off on Barra. She's carried it with her throughout her 40-plus-year career at GM.

It's a great lesson for leaders on how to bring everyone to the table to build a high-performing organization.

Mary Barra started at GM when she was an 18-year-old, working as a college co-op student. Over her long tenure, she's worked on the assembly line as a quality control officer, as an executive assistant, plant manager, HR leader, and several other roles. In 2014, she became the first female CEO of a major automaker.

She rose up the ranks by leading with empathy and taking the perspective of every GM employee. She understood because in several instances, at one point, she had their job. "I also got to see the company and the world from their perspective. Often they would share their dreams and their struggles. I learned empathy—putting myself in their shoes. Empathy . . . it's foundational to any form of leadership."[1]

Not long after Mary Barra first became CEO, GM needed to recall 2.6 million small cars because of a defective ignition switch. The worry was that the engine could shut off while the car was moving. Shockingly, this resulted in 124 deaths.[2] Barra inherited a very challenging situation. Shortly after, she testified before Congress regarding the ignition switch crisis. The way she handled the Congressional testimony was clear, apologetic, and accountable.

She said, "We're going to be transparent. We're going to do everything we can to support the customer. And we're gonna do everything in our power to make sure it never happens again."[3]

Barra's forthright approach to acknowledging responsibility, while working to get better, has carried her and GM forward into a new, innovative era where electric and self-driving cars could shape the course of the automotive industry.

What's differentiated Barra as a champion leader is the human side of leadership she's put in to both her people and GM customers. While delivering the commencement address at Duke University in 2022, she outlined five lessons learned from the kitchen table growing up.[4] They show us the power of coming together and the key ingredients to do so.

1. "Do your best."

A call to work hard. Go after what you're doing with maximum effort.

2. "Find your purpose."

   Discover what kind of leader you are, and know what drives you, as this will help you lead your organization.

3. "Listen to understand."

   The wisest lesson you'll learn as a leader is to ask questions and listen first. As Barra says, "Don't be so proud that you think you have all the answers. Listen."

4. "Be honest, always."

   Always speak the truth and deal in the truth, and be willing to own up to your mistakes.

5. "Include one more. Make room at the table."

   The ethos of Barra's leadership approach is inclusivity and caring for people.

Champion leaders make everyone around them better by tapping into their own unique talents and skills to elevate the unique talents and skills of others. The ability to put yourself in the position of someone, understand them, and lead them along their journey to peak performance is the art of inspiring organizational greatness.

A Story to Tell

> *"Hearing stories acts as a kind of mental flight simulator, preparing us to respond more quickly and effectively."*
>
> —*Chip and Dan Heath*, Made to Stick

Storytelling is about bringing in personal, emotional experiences and sharing them in an authentic way. Chip and Dan Heath highlight the power of emotions and telling stories in their best-selling book *Made to Stick,* which inspires us to communicate in ways that connect with people. Getting people on board with your vision is a lot harder when they don't *feel* it. Deep down, we're yearning for the "good stuff" and the details about who someone is, so we can decide how much we want to let them in or follow them. In leadership, we're always looking to influence someone in an effort to innovate, achieve a goal, build a relationship, or get them to see things from our point of view. As the Heaths write, "How do we get people to care about our ideas? We make them feel something. . . . We are wired to feel things for people, not for abstractions. Sometimes the hard part is finding the right emotion to harness."[5]

I've found the most effective way for leaders to connect is to share personal experiences in a humble, vulnerable way.

Be concise, honest, and add humor when you can. One of the best ways to engage people is through telling a joke or even self-deprecating humor. It humanizes us more and allows someone *inside* to see who we really are. There's something magnetic about watching someone tell a story that brings out their passion and joy. Sharing a joke evokes positive emotions and laughter that leave an indelible mark on our memories. This can carry over to future interactions, as well.

A CEO who I've worked with for several years built cohesion and camaraderie among his senior staff by sharing more pieces of himself and in turn, asking his team more about themselves. Too many leaders think it's a waste of time or that they'd be perceived as full of themselves to share about their families or their life and business lessons learned. But that's where the good stuff is. Those precious moments are your opportunity to authentically lean in and build connection through stories that stick.

Take that chance and relay a story in an all-hands meeting, a town hall, weekly team meetings, and one-on-one conversations. "Read the room" and don't *always* make it about yourself. Be selective because timing matters. You want to connect to the time and feeling of when you were in their position and how you made a decision, identified an opportunity, or learned a lesson that unlocked things for you. In turn, encourage your team members to share stories from their journeys. That's how high-performing teams build empathy and connection.

Empathy leads to servant leadership and a desire to help others. When you tell stories, customize them to meet that person where they're at. And in this *dance* of connection, you may be able to find the right move that leads to someone letting you in to help them.

Telling stories with enthusiasm and precise details helps others to visualize and maybe even see themselves in that situation. Be a teacher! Help your colleagues to learn and see themselves in that story. You want to create an experience that someone else feels a part of, even if they haven't yet experienced it for themselves.

Making a One-on-One Connection

The best way to gain an understanding of your organization's culture is to experience it! This starts with your team, by having conversations with each of your direct reports. From there, you can expand your circle of influence by connecting with individuals in each business unit of your organization. Seek to understand first.

For each individual relationship, it's best to lay the groundwork by establishing rapport. Let each person know they can come to you to ask questions, ask for help, or make a suggestion. You can have all of these things while establishing boundaries to avoid constant interruptions. One-on-one meetings for some teams are only about reviewing tasks. If you find yourself only focused on tasks and deliverables in one-on-one meetings, I encourage you to set up an outline for what the ideal one-on-one meeting looks like (more on this following). There's so much opportunity in one-on-one meetings to listen, get to know someone, share ideas, find out what opportunities they're looking for, and highlight your vision and big-picture strategic priorities.

> **The Ideal One-on-One**
>
> Following the guidance of the preceding words, let's take a five-minute timeout. Get a notebook, or feel free to use a digital notebook or tool. List out the criteria that make up the ideal one-on-one meeting that you'd like to experience as both (a) a team member and (b) a leader. Ask yourself questions such as: What matters most to me? What do I need help with? What do I need to know? How can I best support *this* specific team member? This brainstorm will help you take greater ownership—and partnership—of the meeting agenda, and contribute to making each one-on-one meeting more productive.

And remember this—there doesn't always have to be harmony in every conversation. Don't be afraid to disagree. Don't be afraid to speak up and tell your team member or leader what you need—or what you feel they can do better.

At Netflix, it's considered essential to speak up when you have an idea to share, feedback to provide, or when you disagree with someone else's point of view. Netflix founder and former CEO Reed Hastings says in *No Rules Rules: Netflix and the Culture of Reinvention,* "It's fine to disagree with your manager and implement an idea she dislikes. We don't want people putting aside a great idea because the manager doesn't see how great it is."[6]

Author Erin Meyer adds in *No Rules Rules*, "At Netflix, it is tantamount to being disloyal to the company if you fail to speak up when you disagree with a colleague or have feedback that could be helpful."

While there's no cadence set in stone for one-on-ones, I've found that holding once per week formal check-ins for 30 minutes creates a nice rhythm for connection. Like with anything, if that's not needed, mold this to fit both of your needs. The big thing is to focus on quality and frequency for how you're communicating. Ask open-ended questions that get your employees to share their thoughts. Deliver messages that inspire thought. Share timely pieces of feedback. I encourage you to hold these meetings in-person, when possible, and otherwise to use a video-conferencing tool. Some days, a phone call may suffice, but try and personalize the experience as much as possible.

Begin by asking how the person is doing and how they're feeling. Ask about their family, how their weekend was, or how their overall experience is going. By having more frequent conversations throughout the year, you can learn what they're passionate about, the work they enjoy most, and how they like to spend their time. The best way to meet someone where they're at and truly connect is to try and find shared experiences among the things they enjoy most. This could be personally or professionally—the only way to find out is to ask! Be willing to share pieces of yourself with them. And remember to offer specific help that is tailored to their needs based on what they've already told you. Always find a way to recognize them. Specificity and timing here are key.

Over time, we tend to tune out "Good work!" or "Nice job," because they sound cliché. The way you connect with someone is by recognizing or showing them appreciation with *specific* feedback delivered at the right moments. Applaud them for their effort or positive attitude. Highlight how they explained the nuances of your product during a sales pitch. Some like to call that a compliment. I call it "well-timed praise." Well-timed praise is authentic and individualized to connect with someone's exact experiences and emotions. It's also not done all the time. Be judicious with giving heartfelt recognition. Trust your instincts and know you can do this both one-on-one and in team settings so the group can recognize that person's contributions.

Here is some champion leader guidance for annual reviews and career development conversations:

- Empower directs to add agenda items to meetings;
- Set up guardrails to ensure you're at least holding quarterly career development discussions;
- Ensure there are no surprises by having regular feedback conversations;
- Allow your team members to account for how they feel they've performed;
- Ask open-ended questions, and give each person the opportunity to explain themselves around team-related things they feel have gone well and things that haven't;
- Ensure there are clear action items and goals; and
- Finish on an optimistic note!

The most essential outcome from a meeting is to have a path forward. Notice, I didn't write "consensus." Direction is what is needed. Aim for this beforehand, but recognize that things are fluid. New information comes to light. You want to establish direction that provides everyone with clear, actionable items so everyone knows what they're tasked to do and they're aware of what everyone else is doing.

Influence and Impact

Agility and a willingness to adapt to change creates high performance both short and long term. But let's be honest—there's a whole lot more to the picture than being quick to react and willing to change. Championship organizations are agile. They're always willing to learn from their mistakes *and* use those lessons as the foundation for future growth. If one strategy doesn't work, have a team postmortem to understand why and then decide new, innovative ways to go forward. Ask the tough questions, learn, and *go*!

Agile organizations create a culture of esprit de corps to build high-performing teams who care passionately about each other and the business results they achieve. It becomes challenging to solve tough problems and to innovate when you don't trust each other—and when you lack empathy toward one another. Get to know your people, and invest in them. Velocity matters. The speed in which you execute—without sacrificing quality—delivers high-performance results to your customers, faster. Agile organizations focus on both the process and the end result.

Never lose sight of either. And in the process, remember to find ways to keep things "loose" by building in time for fun team-building activities such as lunches or holiday events.

Brian Chesky, the founder and CEO of Airbnb, has championed the creation of experiences for Airbnb customers. He's led with authenticity and created a community-driven platform that has met the demands and needs of customers. Airbnb has become so much more than just a place to rent a house or room for a brief stay. Chesky's leadership has helped Airbnb establish trust with customers by connecting them to fun, new travel experiences that provide a local touch of hospitality. He's provided a similar, powerful experience for his own employees by empowering them to be serial entrepreneurs. He's given them the opportunity to voice their needs during employee town hall meetings, and he's always created an environment of open, transparent communication.

Take a pulse check and focus on your organization's agility. Reevaluate roles and responsibilities. Put people in the best position to succeed. Hold strategic conversations on a monthly or quarterly basis. The goal here is to be responsive and to have your teams prepared to adapt to change.

When working cross-functionally, have open, honest conversations where your team members can get to know each other. There should be no "strangers" among you. Strategic initiatives fail or succeed based on communication—and the best time to communicate is at the beginning. Where possible, have this take place in person and share experiences with one another.

Cultivating an Organizational Growth Mindset

> *"When entire companies embrace a growth mindset, their employees report feeling far more empowered and committed; they also receive far greater organizational support for collaboration and innovation."*[7]
>
> —Dr. Carol Dweck

Thousands of hours of coaching conversations and team-building workshops have shown me that self-awareness and self-confidence play the biggest roles in an employee's development. When you affirm, validate, and provide constructive feedback to your employees, you will nurture their growth and self-awareness.

Self-confidence is achieved through preparation, hard work, achievement, reminding yourself of your accomplishments, and by cultivating a growth mindset. The latter two areas are where you can significantly improve someone else's confidence, empowering and encouraging their mental and emotional well-being.

Champion leaders know that helping their employees to cultivate a growth mindset is the key to enduring success. This desire to embrace challenges and the ability to execute powers the most successful organizations. As a senior leader at one of the top global tech companies told me about top-performing organizations, "It comes down to skill and will."

For our purposes, let's define *skill* as the composite of talents, learned abilities, and experiences. We can help foster an individual's learning and development and help them improve their skills through training, on-the-job experience, and feedback. The skills and knowledge they bring to the job are acquired through years of effort, practice, and experience. We have more leadership influence over the "will" portion of their continued development. It's directly correlated with confidence, desire, and drive (playing offense) and mitigating insecurity, self-doubt, and fear of failure (playing defense).

Dr. Carol Dweck's seminal research on adopting a growth mindset has taught us about the importance of a lifelong education of learning and perseverance. We know that if we stay static and see our talents and skills as fixed, we diminish our chances for future growth. Worse yet, we may not even give things a try. Your goal is to inspire the growth of each person's mindset so that the collective parts come together for a powerful sum.

I like to look at it this way—if you're positive and optimistic, you're more likely to develop a growth mindset. You can model it, you can teach it, and the goal should be to continuously cultivate this through feedback, development opportunities, and in team meetings. That's how we create the fertile and dynamic conditions for personal development.

Here are five ways to cultivate a growth mindset:

1. Keep a notebook with you at all times and write out positive affirmations. Reread these to yourself each day to lift your spirit.

   What you start for yourself, you can bring out to others. Encourage employees in one-on-one and team meetings. Follow up and send a text, instant message, or email to check in on them. Affirm them throughout the process, not just for the end results.

2. Live with the mantra "What's in the way, is the way," and conquer your biggest fears not by working harder but by managing your thoughts and emotions.

Get your team members to share their biggest fears—their obstacles and impediments to achievement. Then ask them, What can you do to overcome these?

3. Don't blame yourself for mistakes. Success is a team effort. Self-accusation leads to stagnation—meaning you stop or slow down. Forgive yourself. Learn. Move forward.

   Begin your next team meeting by acknowledging a mistake you've made—and share the lesson(s) you learned with everyone.

4. Don't criticize someone. Give them a compliment instead.

   If you feel the inclination to criticize coming on, pause and take a deep breath. One criticism can do more damage than 10 compliments can help. Build a relationship, don't tear one down.

5. Don't obsess over every one of your thoughts. Take the positive ones in and nurture them. See the negative thoughts for what they are. Manage them and move on.

Stop This Culture Killer

The #1 behavior that I've seen destroy team cultures is negative criticism—both what's heard and what isn't. To prevent dissension among the team, set the tone upfront that outward, open criticism of another person is prohibited. You must eliminate this and always call it out when you observe it. Similarly, tell your team that gossip and talking behind people's backs is not allowed. Think about it—there is nothing good that comes from either of these things. They lack integrity and completely dissolve trust. Root these out right away. Always replace a negative criticism or gossip with a positive contribution. Turn it around!

Keep your focus—and your team's focus—on the next step in front of you. You cannot change the past. Live in the present, with an eye for the future.

Creating a Culture of Connection

So what is culture? I define culture as "the values, beliefs, synergies, commitment to excellence, and camaraderie that serves as the enduring heartbeat of the organization."

Creating a culture of connection starts with the level of emotional equity you put in. Caring for your employees' well-being and success is paramount. From there, you build from the individual to the organizational success and well-being. Care—empathy in action—helps you retain your top performers and create an enduring, rewarding partnership that leads to growth and results. I've developed four actionable and practical ways you can create a compassionate, sustainable, and supportive culture that everyone wants to be a part of. Start here.

1. Care for Your Employees

> *"People don't care how much you know until they know how much you care."*
>
> —Theodore Roosevelt

The wisdom of President Theodore Roosevelt's quote is at the heart of empathy and shows us that caring for your people is rooted in desire. This is entirely within your control. You have to want it! It's the difference between transactional leadership and transformational leadership. Transactional leadership is just that—a transaction with a need and a timestamp attached to it. Clear results and expectations are provided, usually with rewards or punishments attached.

Short-term, this isn't always bad. When things need to get done quickly, sometimes a direct, telling style is needed. But it's lacking in the personalized touch that empathy provides, which leads to longer-term results and stronger relationships.

Caring for people takes time. It starts *local*, with you. Understand the importance of respect when building trust. When you respect others, you'll be respected more. Here are two examples of organizations doing it right: Deloitte has "care" woven into the fabric of their core values, specifically citing "Take care of each other." Olympus highlights *empathy* and *unity* as two of its core values that demonstrate a care for all stakeholders and the strength in coming together as a team.

Think of the genius of the show *Undercover Boss*, and see how you can mimic this in your workplace. Do a job shadow of employees by specific roles in your organization. Spend half a day shadowing the employees as they work. Ask insightful questions, inquire what they need to perform their jobs better, and see whether there are ways you can connect teams cross-functionally to solve problems and help one another. How you spend your time is a direct reflection of what you value. People know when you care—they see it when you're by their side supporting them.

2. Listen to Your Employees

When you're forming a team, it's easy to think the only way you can connect with someone is by relating to them with a shared experience. But what happens when that isn't there? What do you do then? Start by listening. It's better to have a beginner's mind, to understand someone, and the emotions they express, when they're sharing pieces of themselves. This is why empathy matters—it invites us to listen and to let curiosity guide us.

Harvard professor Dr. Francesca Gino writes in *Harvard Business Review*, "When we demonstrate curiosity about others by asking questions, people like us *more* and view us as *more* competent, and the heightened trust makes our relationships more interesting and intimate. By asking questions, we promote more-meaningful connections and more-creative outcomes."[8]

The challenge for some leaders is simply to maintain presence, avoid interrupting, and acknowledge the person they're communicating with. Remember—listen, no judgment, no "Yeah, when I . . ." and no problem solving. When you insert yourself too early, when it's not needed, you do more harm than good. Be there in the arena with that person, and look them in the eye. Be patient and ask open-ended questions, rather than close-ended ones. You want to avoid "boxing someone into a corner" by leaving them to only respond with yes, no, good, or OK.

Also, I encourage you to avoid asking questions that begin with "Why" as they can be perceived as accusatory or judgmental. Examples of open-ended questions include:

- How was your weekend?
- What do you feel is best?
- What could we improve?
- What are the obstacles to success?

Communication begins with listening. As a leader, that starts with you. Have an awareness toward recognizing someone's body language—and be aware of your own. Avoid crossing your arms, and be mindful of any facial gestures that express too much skepticism. Be open to receiving someone. Perceive how they take you in. Are they just nodding their head and smiling? Or are they really listening? I truly believe, we know when someone is listening to us and when they're not. We all want to feel heard and acknowledged, so lead with this in mind.

Questions for reflection:

- How can you create a more inclusive environment in your organization?
- What can you do to help your team maintain focus?
- How do you connect best with people in one-on-one meetings?
- What characteristics of having a growth mindset most resonate with you today? What do you want to add going forward?

3. Show Vulnerability and Model Servant Leadership

Vulnerability was scorned or looked on as a sign of weakness for a long time. Not anymore. Champion leaders embrace this mindset and share it with their employees. Share more of yourself with your employees to let them know they can comfortably share pieces of themselves with you. I ask you to think about that professional vulnerability and what you want to let people in on. You get to decide that. You can choose to share about your family, hobbies, and interests. But don't feel you *need* to share every personal part of yourself. It's up to you. People are looking for personalized connection—the camaraderie that helps them feel more a part of things. Look to learn from them! You don't have the ability to hear every conversation or know exactly how work is being executed on the ground level. Learn more about the innovation being done, what your team is working on, and how they're collaborating.

I think back to the gentleman who hired me for my first job in management consulting. He was a very senior-level leader who was an unassuming, quiet man. He knew when to share a story or an example that made us feel more at ease, and it left an indelible impact on the way I treat others. He put himself out there, vulnerable and humble, and never expected much in return.

He went out of his way to meet everyone that he managed and took them out to lunch early on during their tenure with the company. He put people first, surrounded himself with a loving family, kept things positive, and treated others with kindness.

4. Let Go of Control

I've learned throughout all of my relationships that having true power often requires us to cede control to others. When we do this, we enable others to exercise their mental muscles and employ their own brilliance in action. We allow them to play the game the way they were meant to play it.

The more we relinquish control and the notion that we know all the answers, the better we are. This logic is counterintuitive to many people. How could we be more powerful and influential when we are not the ones in control? Pride and ego can cloud our minds, as pride is anathema to developing a beginner's mind.

However, we grow by putting others first. We strengthen our willingness to trust because we are implicitly trusting others to be themselves. Impact comes through kindness, empowerment, and by understanding an individual's needs and wants and then leading them in that direction. When you know this, you're able to help each person achieve their potential.

High-Performing Teams' "Core Four"

High-performing teams have commonalities that help them to consistently achieve results and work well with one another. Here are four in particular that I've found in many organizations.

Focus on the Moment

Focusing on the task at hand with full presence is vitally important. High-performing teams never look too far ahead and don't get caught wondering about the past. They prepare and execute with commitment and high energy.

Fidelity Investments CEO Abby Johnson said, "Every day, you have to get up with new energy and new ideas to contribute to pushing the organization forward . . . a relentless focus on continuing to try to improve everything you do."[9]

Shut out all distractions. The key to championship leadership is to bring everyone together for a common goal, to focus on the task at hand, and execute to the best of your ability.

Check the "Little Things"

The "little things" are the crucial details that determine the outcomes of business deals, tasks, projects, and long-term team success. This can come down to micro-level details such as holding a five-minute meeting to ensure everyone's on the same page or thanking a team member for a contribution. The "little things" aren't, well, little at all. They're the tremendously important words and actions that make a difference in your team succeeding. These "little things" don't just happen by chance or luck.

Earlier in my career in management consulting, I saw a multimillion-dollar deal completed because my team took the time to meticulously proofread every detail of the proposal. We captured everything 100% accurately. Our competitor did not.

I cannot stress enough how important it is to cover all bases. Come up with your own list of what these things are. Speeches can motivate, and emotional language can inspire. But those things alone do not build high-performing teams. Smart, disciplined work, a positive attitude, and a willingness to do all the "little things" that focus on results, team-building, and innovation are what create a winner.

Look at your team. Ask yourself, "Am I doing everything that I can to be great? Or am I only focusing on certain core areas?" A comprehensive checkup of your team will allow you to identify all of the methods and actions you can integrate into your repertoire so that it will show up when it counts.

Commit to a Goal

High-performing teams begin each project or fiscal year with very specific end goals in mind. In business, it could be reaching a new revenue goal or adding a new product to the line. A goal can also be an improvement, in terms of profit, reaching key metrics or personal development goals from the year before.

Metrics for human resource (HR)–related items could be:

- Time to hire;
- Employee net promoter score (eNPS);
- Employee turnover rate; and
- Employee engagement.

I find that these are excellent ways to track your HR-related goals and keep you on track. You likely know the challenges or key areas to focus on in your organization. When you take inventory and plan for team success, leave no stone unturned. Brainstorm all of the things you need to do in order to be successful. Then, have an overarching main goal, along with several other subgoals you aspire to accomplish. Measure yourself against these goals to make sure your performance is in line with your expectations.

Control Attitude and Effort

There are two things you can always control: your attitude and your effort.

Having a positive attitude means being willing to do whatever it takes to make your teammates and yourself better. It means showing up and leading at your best. A positive attitude produces mental toughness, which leads to perseverance and taking accountability for your performance.

Hard work, or maximum effort, guides you to get the job done and be there for others. It means spotting opportunities and risks and looking out for your team to support them through every challenging moment. If you rely on this approach, you will see positive results. Everyone meets with temporary defeat, on occasion, but persistent, perseverant people power through by relying on a positive attitude and determined work ethic. The more people you have on your team who embody these qualities, the greater your chances are at reaching your goals.

Your Organization Exercise

Gather your team together, and ask each person to come up with crucial, small details that they feel end up making a *big* difference in team success. These are really the "little things" that can become the backbone of your team creed. The beauty of this exercise is to get feedback from each team member. Encourage them to share stories and experiences of moments that lifted them up and helped lead to collaboration. Be specific and speak from the heart.

Champion's Checklist (Tools and Takeaways)

- ☑ Gain alignment, and ensure there is understanding after every meeting.
- ☑ Acknowledge each employee's ideas and inputs; factor these into decisions and opportunities.
- ☑ Live each day with a growth mindset, and give this gift to your team by inspiring them to live with a growth mindset.
- ☑ Keep a journal of "well-timed praise" that you can give to your team members.
- ☑ Recognize that giving up control and being vulnerable is about being self-aware, confident—and being yourself.

Chapter 5

Prioritization (*Master the Art of Time Management and Strategy*)

"Only having a certain number of hours in the day have really forced me to prioritize. I focused on the things that are the biggest impact."

—Susan Wojcicki

Whether you're leading a family or an organization—or both—figuring out the balance of work and life is a challenge that every one of us faces. Long commutes, work-from-home routines, ensuring we're organized and our to-do lists are ready to go—these all factor into how we tackle each day. A champion leader who has artfully navigated this balance throughout her career is former YouTube CEO Susan Wojcicki.

Before retiring from her role as CEO in early 2023, Wojcicki became an icon of women tech leaders everywhere for her industry expertise, promotion of work-life balance, and innovative strategies that continue to lead YouTube into a new era. She's also a mother of five children who built an incredibly successful career as a working mother. The keys to her success? Prioritizing time with her family and keeping high-impact things at the forefront of her work.

She also played a unique role in a famous backstory.

In the late summer of 1998, she and her husband rented the garage of their Silicon Valley home to a couple of 25-year-old computer scientists. You may know them better as Google cofounders Larry Page and Sergey Brin. It was there in Wojcicki's garage that Google was born. She later became the 16th Google employee. Wojcicki played a gigantic role in the future success of Google. She was responsible for developing the advertising product AdWords and also advocating for Google to acquire YouTube in 2006. Smart move. Acquired for $1.65 billion, it's estimated that YouTube could be worth more than $300 billion today.

Wojcicki's time with her family gives her fulfillment, renews her mind, and sharpens her focus.

She said, "When I come back to work, I actually have a better understanding of what needs to get done, and things that seemed really important suddenly don't seem as important two days later. When I get really frustrated with something, I just stop doing it."[1]

Knowing how to prioritize enabled Wojcicki to elevate YouTube to new heights. Prioritizing responsibilities inspired her to be fresh and fully present at the office. Part of that strategy? Going home on most days at 6 p.m. to eat dinner and spend time with her family and not checking email during those special hours. Wojcicki has been a huge champion of flexible work hours and taking breaks and paid maternity leave, which have helped Google to attract and retain more women.

She said: "I believe that taking breaks, having the opportunity to reflect and renew, actually gives you more firepower when you're in the office. In a field like technology that requires a lot of innovation, if you are burnt out, it's hard to continue to innovate and have that inspiration."[2]

I'm a father of three young boys, so these words carry the greatest resonance and weight. Taking breaks, finding time to reflect, and thinking strategically are the master tools of leaders who prioritize their time. In this chapter, you'll learn exactly how to become more efficient with your time to have the greatest influence. And remember, the evolution needed to become a champion leader starts with the vision of seeing people as your top priority.

Setting Yourself Up for Success

My favorite quote on time comes from Apple cofounder and former CEO Steve Jobs: "It's really clear that the most precious resource we all have is time."

The most commonly heard words I hear on time are these: "I don't have the time."

Yes.

You.

Do.

This is fact, not opinion. This subtle mindset change will shift the paradigm for how you view your days, weeks, and months. It will get you to think deeper on how you choose to spend this most precious resource. It's truly a matter of prioritization. All of us will have days—perhaps consecutive days—in "back-to-back meetings" focused on business results. That's to be expected. But if you find yourself in this position every day, with no time for your team or strategic thinking, it's time to reconsider how you plan your day.

The most powerful time prioritization and productivity tool I use with clients is the Eisenhower Matrix, which gives us a framework to become more efficient by determining what is most important and urgent. You can use this for yourself and also with your team. Either way, the best place to begin is organizing your priorities by importance.

One example is to see your tasks and meetings through these three areas: innovation, teamwork, and results. Start here and think about how things stack for you. You can also develop your own criteria. Let's look at several areas (among many) of what's most important for you as a leader (in no particular order):

- Growth;
- People;
- Communication;
- Vision and strategy;
- Excellence of results;
- Quality of products, ideas, and offerings;
- Financial performance;
- Leadership;
- Hiring and retaining employees;
- Developing new products, ideas, and offerings;
- Teamwork;
- Culture;
- Cultivating new leaders; and
- Advancement opportunities.

Getting Clear on What Matters (and What Doesn't) with the Eisenhower Matrix

Now, let's dive into the matrix, shown in Figure 5.1.

Your starting point for properly using the Eisenhower Matrix to your team's advantage is to first define what is urgent and important, as shown in the first quadrant. I encourage you to begin with importance, which will tie back to your vision, purpose, mission, and strategic goals. This should be an inclusive process that receives input from many stakeholders and is pressure-tested by variables such as time, effort, and impact.

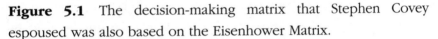

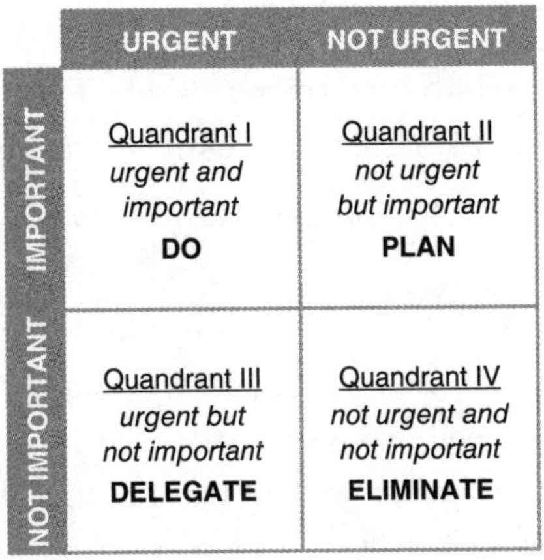

URGENT
NOT URGENT
IMPORTANT
NOT IMPORTANT
Quandrant I
urgent and important
DO
Quandrant II
not urgent but important
PLAN
Quandrant III
urgent but not important
DELEGATE
Quandrant IV
not urgent and not important
ELIMINATE

Figure 5.1 The decision-making matrix that Stephen Covey espoused was also based on the Eisenhower Matrix.

Source: Davidjcmorris, https://commons.wikimedia.org/wiki/File:7_habits_decision-making_matrix.png.

So what does it mean to define importance? The answer should be: "By doing these things, we will deliver maximum value to our organization and those we serve." This is unique to each organization. "Important" comes first. At a strategic level, that definition guides you to set the tactical things that you need to accomplish.

Urgency determines the order for when things need to be completed. Where I see some leaders struggle is thinking "the next fire" or "shiny object" is what needs their immediate attention. You safeguard against this by balancing urgency with importance. In the broader view, it's best to have an *intake system*. This means that every time a new strategic initiative, project, or task comes in, your team has a repeatable process geared toward efficiency and quality to help you plan, delegate, and execute.

Consider these factors for your intake system:

- Define the level of importance, when it's due, who it's for, and who the request is coming from;
- Evaluate how much time it will take;

- Determine risks and dependencies;
- Decide who will be the owner or directly responsible individual (DRI); and team members assigned to the work; and
- Put a date on when you expect this to be completed.

Having an intake system gives you more control and influence over how you manage each new priority. It helps you stay organized, knowing that plans will always change. Choose what you need to own, what you can partner with others on, and what you can delegate to others. I call this "Own, Partner, Delegate." This can form the backbone of your intake system and prepare you for what comes next. Now, let's take a more detailed look at each quadrant of the Eisenhower Matrix.

Quadrant I: Urgent and Important (Do)

Let's be real—we usually *know* right away what a quadrant I item is. It's work in our main area of responsibility that normally has a clear date and time attached to it. Sometimes, it's an emergency that needs to be dealt with. The big thing to beware of in quadrant I is operating in a perpetual mode of fire drills. This can happen in fast-paced organizations. It's imperative to get your team's culture out of fire-fighting mode—where everything is considered urgent and important—and into a more balanced style where you're able to strategically delegate.

Attrition and hiring freezes all play a role in speeding up the pace and workload that can fall on many employees' shoulders. No matter your leadership role in the organization, it's critical to ask questions and use an intake system to determine priority. I encourage you to take ownership of your intake system and push back on requests that you deem to be nonurgent. You want to have autonomy to make decisions and determine what your team takes on and what they don't. This can be risky, and I encourage you to do so respectfully, but it's also a hallmark of a champion leader.

When you've done your due diligence to know what is most important and what is urgent, you should feel confident in asserting yourself to question what needs to be done right away. For example, in a technology organization, meeting the time deadline on a new, emerging product for a global launch is a clear quadrant I item, as are any bug fixes that need to follow. Long-term, any organization whose team members are perpetually functioning in quadrant I will burn out. On top of it, if you're short-staffed, you'll need to be even more agile in how you balance priorities. How you schedule urgent tasks and delegate these effectively will very often determine your success as a team.

Quadrant II: Not Urgent but Important (Plan)

Quadrant II is exactly where strategic prioritization takes place. This is where you dive into the biggest impact items. Planning (or as I like to call it, *strategy*) leads to top-notch execution. Quadrant II is where champion leaders spend a lot of their time. This is where relationship building, process improvement, goal setting, creative thinking, and learning take place. To paraphrase Al Pacino in *Any Given Sunday*, it's a game of inches, and champion leaders are willing to fight for that inch. These "inches" are *why* we prioritize our time. It's where you get to know yourself better and how you strategize to lift others up. As you'll see from the wisdom of Indra Nooyi, in Chapter 8, it's also where you get "out in the field."

As a leader, you have the privilege to decide each week what the highest quality and highest impact activities are that are not constrained by deadlines. Plan them in. As President Dwight Eisenhower said, "Plans are nothing. Planning is everything." Plans will change. You'll need to improvise and adapt, but your guiding principles will lead you back to finding a way to build in time for what's most important.

You're best able to accomplish this balance through time-blocking. This means carving in specific, free-flowing periods of time on your calendar that prioritize high-impact activities. Be protective of your time—frankly, it's the only area of management where I encourage leaders to be greedy. When you're able to concentrate on what's most important, you're able to innovate, see the big picture, and challenge conventional ways of thinking. The key here is seeing quadrant II as your most valuable time and not to postpone it for a day that may never come.

Paul Graham, a venture capitalist, computer scientist, and entrepreneur, wrote about using a unique approach to how we see our time, which he labeled: "maker's schedule, manager's schedule."[3] Managers are more likely to manage time by the hour, as in a traditional appointment schedule, which is logical when having many meetings. Makers try to build in occasional free-flowing time in the mornings or afternoons that are free of interruptions. Even one meeting can greatly affect or disrupt creative rhythm, so it's better to have free-flowing time to think strategically. This emphasis on strategic time is one of the key drivers for setting a long-term direction for your organization. It helps you to stay proactive, rather than reactive.

Another big part of staying proactive strategically is having conversations that generate ideas. Maybe your conversation with the manufacturing floor worker makes the difference in improving the quality of your product. Maybe those extra hours talking to customers help shape the vision of a future product. Sara Blakely's genius in building Spanx into a billion-dollar company came from conversations she had in department stores with prospective customers. She literally got the voice of the customer directly. It's made all the difference in creating a product engineered to the exact specifications of women around the globe.

Quadrant III: Urgent but Not Important (Delegate)

As Warren Buffett once said, "The difference between successful people and very successful people is that very successful people say 'no' to almost everything."

There's a balance between knowing what to say no to and understanding the things that no longer rise to your level of significance as a leader. I encourage you to view quadrant III through this lens. Obviously, if something were categorically unimportant, it wouldn't be worth getting done at all. By defining what is most important for you and your team, you're also defining what isn't important. You're able to determine things that may not be important enough for you to own but are within the scope of importance to delegate to others.

Delegation is a strategic decision. When you see it this way, you realize that letting go of tasks and empowering people to complete them maximizes everyone's time. As a leader, your sole focus is not on execution. It's on developing your employees, meeting their needs, and helping eliminate obstacles and challenges from their path. It's on identifying new opportunities and putting resources into improving your product, service, or delivery.

The art of delegating is an up-front time investment that must be consistently met for long-term success. You'll end up spending more time in this phase, but you'll save a lot of time in the long run. It's a quid pro quo. Invest more time in the short term for greater efficiency, balance, and productivity in the long term. It's an investment worth making.

Situational Leadership® is an outstanding framework to use for delegating tasks to your team members and adapting your leadership style to fit their exact needs.[4] It begins with assessing the Performance Readiness® Level of the individual you're delegating to. Meaning, you want to know if they're able to complete a *task*. And you want to understand their motivation, mindset, or confidence level for taking on a specific task. The Performance Readiness Levels include:

- R1: Unable and unwilling/insecure;
- R2: Unable but willing/confident;
- R3: Able but unwilling/insecure; and
- R4: Able and willing/confident.

By understanding our employees' skill and will we're better positioned to set someone up for success and delegate effectively. This factors into knowing what to delegate and what not to delegate as a leader. Each Performance Readiness corresponds with a leadership style. These are:

- S1: Telling, directing, or guiding;
- S2: Selling, coaching, or explaining;
- S3: Participating, collaborating, or facilitating; and
- S4: Delegating, empowering, or monitoring.

In other words, if someone is unable to do a task but demonstrates the confidence to want to learn, we want to meet them with a selling, coaching, or explaining style (S2 meets the R2). Focus on matching up each number on the "R" side with the corresponding number on the "S" side (e.g., R1 to S1).

You might be wondering, What should I delegate and what should I not?

Things to delegate include the following:

- Tactical work that is more day-to-day;
- Work that will develop the skills and confidence of your team;
- Meetings that don't require executive-level decisions;
- Work your team will enjoy; and
- Tasks that challenge them that don't require your direction.

Things *not* to delegate include the following:

- Most important tasks tied to strategic goals;
- Tasks or meetings tied to your core responsibilities;
- Strategic, executive-level decisions; and
- Very urgent tasks that will take too long to explain.

Now, let's move on to what we can eliminate.

Quadrant IV: Not Urgent and Not Important (Eliminate)

Some things are better to put in the trash bin. Most leaders aren't focused on things that are unimportant. But it's always valuable to reassess meetings and tasks from time to time to see whether you should eliminate things that are redundant, unnecessary, or not yielding value. I encourage you to follow the principle of knowing what to say no to (more on this in Chapter 7), and if you find things no longer have the importance they once did, remove them.

Here are tasks or meetings that you can eliminate as a leader:

- Administrative tasks that provide no value;
- Meetings where your feedback or viewpoint is not needed;

- Old projects or items that no longer tie to strategic priorities; and
- Time wasters that detract from your high-priority initiatives.

Putting Together the Quadrants

I come back to my background in management consulting and project management to identify the five phases of the project management life cycle as defined by the Project Management Institute (PMI):[4]

- Initiating;
- Planning;
- Executing;
- Monitoring and Controlling; and
- Closing.

Where many organizations get it wrong is thinking they can just jump into the execution phase of things in quadrant I. Without putting in the initiating, planning and prioritization work that comes in quadrant II, you aren't able to see things strategically. Be a chess player, and don't just play checkers. Prioritize to ensure you're adequately staffed and that deliverables have been scoped from a time, cost, and quality perspective. This puts you in better position to execute. Again, this means making an up-front time investment that gives you strategic direction.

This becomes a mindset that helps you to see the field more evenly. Reserving time for this and seeing it as important, while admittedly not urgent, is a foundational pillar of championship leadership. You have to carve in the time to your calendar! Huge successes don't take place without doing the work before the work, so to speak. As pressures and workload increase, it gets harder to make the time. But you should always do it.

Questions for reflection:

- How much time per week can I devote to ad hoc and planned conversations both in one-on-one and group sessions?
- What tasks or initiatives no longer rise to my level of significance as a leader, and should be delegated to my team?
- What habits do I want to create to help me become more disciplined with my time?
- What do I see as my quadrant II tasks (personally and professionally)?

The Classification of Your Time

What has worked wonders for my clients, and helped me exponentially as an entrepreneur, is classifying my time into categories. I call mine "the 3 C's":

- **Clients:** My top focus as an executive coach, consultant and keynote speaker is the clients I serve. I want to know them, understand their needs, and do everything in my power to serve them. Clients come first.
- **Creativity:** Creativity is what made writing this book possible. I'm an author who writes books and speeches, prepares team-building workshops, and contributes thought leadership to thousands of organizations. I also created the LinkedIn Learning course "*Leading with Emotional Intelligence.*" Creativity is where I spend a lot of my time.
- **Create new business:** Creating new business is the lifeblood of every entrepreneur and every successful organization. Marketing, sales, and understanding who needs my services is another way to prioritize my time.

You may be the CEO of a large entertainment company. You may be a senior executive for a pharmaceutical company. You may be an entrepreneur yourself, leading a start-up for a new tech company. My message to you is: find *your* 3 C's. Create your own classification for how you prioritize your time. Come up with a simple mnemonic that you can always turn to that helps you stay organized. The key is to choose something that becomes a part of your subconscious memory and is easily recalled.

Whether that's the 3 C's, an acronym, or even a name, use something that helps you classify the majority of your most important work.

Having the Discipline for "Locking It In"

We have the power to carry out daily tasks, achieve goals, and improve the connection of our teams. Our self-discipline is influenced by our emotional self-regulation, habits, and our motivation. The reason many leaders and managers don't actually lock in time comes down to not seeing it as a priority. It's seen as one extra thing to do. But if we're able to use tools such as digital calendars and apps to serve as reminders, we have a much better shot of getting something done.

Neuroscientist Richard Sima writes, "Perhaps even without realizing it, many of us employ a psychological strategy called cognitive offloading, where we use a physical action to reduce demands on our brain. When we outsource our intentions from being stored just in our brains to somewhere outside our head—a notepad, Google Calendar, or alerts on our smartphones—we are performing a specific kind of cognitive offloading known as intention offloading."[5]

"Locking it in" is made possible through intention offloading. It's the creation of a system, and it's this system that serves as the foundation for accomplishment as a leader.

Locking it in is not complicated. You just need to put an appointment on your calendar with a reminder for it to be done. If it classifies into one of your top three areas (see the previous section), then you know you need to do it. I encourage leaders to have a system for themselves first and then a prioritization structure for their teams. You have to begin with *you* to be organized for others—just like self-awareness serves as the foundation for self-management (see Chapter 2).

Having daily check-ins with yourself is a built-in accountability mechanism that allows you to check progress. Always prioritize first by importance, which is informed by your classification. That leads us to strategy.

Making Time for Strategy

As Ellie Pidot, vice president of strategy at Medtronic, has said, "Strategy is a fancy word for coming up with a long-term plan and putting it into action."

We need strategic direction to know what is—and what isn't—a good use of our time. We have to learn to say no to time wasters. Strategy really is just a fancy word for planning. Strategy clarifies and tells us what matters. Once we know what matters, we can plan our days, weeks, and lives around these most important parts. (Figure 5.2 shows the five stages of time management.)

Planning isn't sexy. Let's get that out of the way. It's not going to give you results now. So as a result, many people don't do it. Instant-gratification thinking clashes with the real world. It's a lie. Results often come many steps after the original idea and planning steps that we've taken.

It's only when we begin to plan and exercise patience, and couple that with the experience of living, that we understand this. It's much harder to rely on our memory alone and achieve big results. Planning gives us the confidence that we need, it helps us prioritize, and gives us an affirmative feeling of positivity that we are well organized and structured.

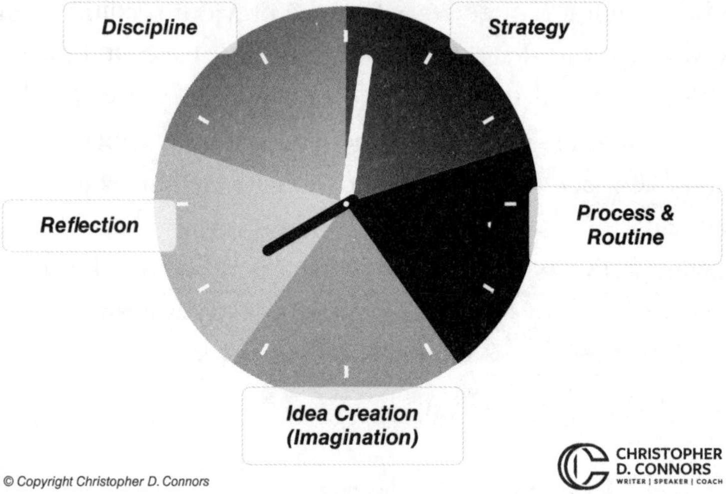

Figure 5.2 Five stages of time management.
Source: Christopher D. Connors.

When you're looking to set your daily, weekly, and monthly strategy, I hope you can build in time for both personal and professional pursuits. Building in time for me comes back to using time blocks on my calendar. I label these by color-coding categories to determine how I'm spending my time. Examples of this for you could be:

- Business development;
- Work execution;
- Fun;
- Learning and development;
- Physical health;
- Family time;
- Ideas and innovation;
- Relationship building; and
- Customer strategy.

The biggest key when it comes to strategy is building in quality time. Do your monthly strategy at the end of each month on a Sunday evening. This ties back to your strategic goals. Weekly strategy sets the tone for your week and focuses on your strategic approach. Only later should you focus tactically on things that will comprise your to-do list.

Schedule your weekly strategy time on the weekend where you're free from the distractions and pressures of the week. Our focus is sharper when we're not dealing with time pressure, stress, or the responsibility of feeling like we need to be somewhere. Plus, there's a good chance you'll have more going on during the week. Set time on a Saturday or Sunday, and this will set the tone for your days ahead. If you've been sluggish getting back into the mix on Mondays, the discipline of having time blocks and a set list of to-do's for the week will help you to create psychological commitment to complete what you need to get done.

For me, Sunday nights around 8:15 work best. Ask yourself, "What works best for me?" You may prefer the mornings. If so, I also recommend Sundays to think clearly and process thoughts away from the rigors of the week.

Daily strategy can have a bigger-picture focus (and often will), but it's better reserved for validating and reprioritizing your tasks and goals for the day. Use this strategic time to reframe expectations and revisit your weekly strategy to ensure you're on the right track. If you needed to carry over some tasks from the day before, this is the time to look at those and determine exactly when you will do them. Think of this as your daily stand-up.

Strategy is your path to business peace of mind. Look at your week. Ask yourself if you can spare two hours. You can break that out in 20-minute increments over six days, while still taking one day off. Twenty minutes per day to brainstorm strategically. Commit. Commit. Commit.

Children, a demanding job, a tough commute, busy social life, multiple projects to juggle? The more the demands, the greater the need to plan. When you take a high-level view of your week and begin to drill down to each day, you realize you can cut out time wasters such as watching TV, surfing the web on your smartphone, and texting with your friends. Where there's a will, there's a way.

Prioritizing Time for Connection

As discussed in *People Come First*, the top priorities for every HR organization are how to

- Attract the best people;
- Engage people; and
- Retain people.

Your connection time with each prospective employee begins with your first electronic, verbal, or in-person touchpoint. Once someone is hired into your organization, prioritizing time in one-on-one and team conversations on career development and well-being will help to build engagement and foster trust.

Employees are looking for work flexibility, professional development opportunities, and an employer who recognizes work-life balance.

If you've created the kind of culture where someone knows they feel valued, you have created a lasting connection.

Prioritizing conversations with your team members gets everyone on the same page. This:

- Helps bring to light both urgent and important items;
- Enables teams to be more strategic and less tactical;

- Improves the quality and frequency of communication between leaders and employees; and
- Creates built-in feedback time.

Connection is the best. There's no question about it; this is a time commitment. But I ask you to think about your desire to serve your employees and customers. If you're willing to put yourself in their shoes, I'd imagine you'd tell me you desire a first-class experience in terms of service, surely, but also a personalized touch with a smile, sincerity, and kindness in how you're treated. So the real questions I ask you are, "Are you willing to make that time investment for your own people? Are you willing to look at what you're doing today with clear eyes and honesty and say, 'Is this good enough *or* do I need to make more time for my team?'"

Habits and Flow

Years ago, at the gym I went to there was a sign on the door that read, "Half the battle is showing up." It's exactly what I think of any time I think about committing something to habit. You cannot form a habit if you don't bother showing up in the first place. That's what discipline is all about. When your discipline is connected to inspiration and a motivational driver, you're putting yourself in a position to create a repeatable process.

As Mihaly Csikszentmihalyi wrote in *Flow*, "The first step is to develop the habit of doing whatever needs to be done with concentrated attention, with skill rather than inertia."[6]

We're at our best when we focus on one thing at a time, in short bursts of concentrated, focused work. When you're in flow, it's as if time has stopped. Everything else (like stress!) doesn't matter anymore. This allows our brain to do less busy work, such as worrying, and helps us hone in on what's most important.

Deep focus and concentration help us to visualize and do the work we want to accomplish. By quieting your mind and fully immersing yourself in the moment, you're able to increase your motivation. To stay in flow, focus intently on what you're doing with full presence. See yourself accomplishing what's in front of you. I've found visualization to be one of the most powerful habit-setting tools that significantly increases our confidence, motivation, and ability to get things done.

Imagine a healthy, productive conversation with an employee that you haven't always after seen eye to eye with. See yourself walking out of the room sharing a laugh and a positive path forward.

Habits lead to productivity. Habits breed consistency and prevent your mind from wandering, worrying, and stressing out over things that don't matter. This gives you more creative time, more time to rest, and time for leisure. Habits form the cornerstone for a productive life, and they fuel the planning that is needed to propel you forward. Always make sure you give yourself a reward for each habit that you set. This is a smart incentive that increases your motivation and the probability that you will maintain the discipline needed to form the habit.

In his book *Tiny Habits*, B.J. Fogg writes, "In order to design successful habits and change your behaviors, you should do three things. Stop judging yourself. Take your aspirations and break them down into tiny behaviors. Embrace mistakes as discoveries and use them to move forward."[7]

You want to focus with discipline and consistency so that you can convert conscious actions into subconscious behaviors. Build in rewards for yourself. This will help you sustain the drive to come back each day with greater motivation.

See yourself in each process. Accept mistakes, and don't get discouraged. It's the discipline and perseverance of trying again that helps us form exceptional habits.

Vision and Reflection

Leaders calmly process each day's activities and ask the questions: What worked well? What didn't? What mistakes were made? Where are the opportunities for improvement? These are the questions on the mind of a constantly self-improving time manager.

One way to reflect throughout your day is to have a separation of time (even five minutes) between meetings, particularly when those meetings are scheduled back-to-back over a long stretch. You need time to process information and regroup to be able to maximize your focus and attention for each new conversation.

A big part of reflection is letting things go and being able to compartmentalize your emotions, accepting each day's results and moving forward with self-assurance, and then, renewing our minds to come back tomorrow with greater energy, effort, and excitement. Enthusiasm is part of reflection. We should always enjoy *some* part of our day. Our attitude is in our control. This helps us with acceptance.

Reflection boosts self-awareness and helps improve self-regulation by having a space to process our emotions and let go of stress from the day. It helps us to glean new insights from our experiences each day. It's a great way for you to finish processing your thoughts from the day and to build momentum for the next one.

That Dreaded Word: Email

One critical insight I've learned in working with thousands of global leaders is that spending too much in your email inbox is a huge time waster. There are more effective ways to get your message out and to be informed. So what to do? Consider using a communication platform, video-based messaging, and text messages that are concise, clear, and personalized. If you're going to use email, be clear, succinct, and indicate when and whether you need a response. Birchbox cofounder and CEO Katia Beauchamp says: "I insist that people on the Birchbox team indicate when they need a response in all emails. It makes prioritization so much faster."[8]

Another great strategy is to use email batching. Set appointments on your calendar to check email three or four times per day for a set period of 15 minutes per time. Set up email notifications for people that require an urgent response. Otherwise, insist that you be contacted by text or a phone call if it's truly urgent. This will help you communicate more efficiently and focus on your highest-impact activities.

Tools

Plenty of tools will help you prioritize, manage your time effectively, and stay focused on your important tasks. Listed here are some of my preferred options. Discover what works for you!

Schedule management and email management tools include the following:

- Microsoft Outlook;
- iCalendar (Apple); and
- Google Calendar.

To-do list tools include the following:

- Pen and paper (analog);
- Digital:
  - Todoist;
  - Evernote;

- OneNote;
- Asana;
- Trello; and
- OmniFocus.

Tools to help with procrastination/focus include the following:

- Focus To-Do;
- Productive-Habit Tracker; and
- Freedom.

Mindfulness tools include the following:

- Insight Timer;
- Calm; and
- Headspace.

Prioritization Exercise

Use "Own, Partner, Delegate" to look at your overall scope of responsibilities. It's as simple as it sounds. This will help you get clear on the priorities you need to own, and inspire a collaborative approach toward partnering and delegating with others.

Champion's Checklist (Tools and Takeaways)

- ☑ Don't just "jump in" to the execution phase. Carve in time for *strategy*.
- ☑ Follow Susan Wojcicki's lead and build in "do not disturb" time for yourself each evening to "turn off" work.
- ☑ Develop your own classification system—make it something easy-to-remember.
- ☑ Block at least one afternoon or morning per month to brainstorm big-picture goals.
- ☑ Reevaluate each month to see whether there's something you can get rid of to give yourself time back.

Chapter 6

Camaraderie (*Create a Team-First Culture*)

"We look each other in the eye. We tell each other the truth. And we trust each other. . . . Don't take your culture for granted. There needs to be a constant renewal of values that lead to camaraderie."

—Mike Krzyzewski

Rejected by every talent agency in Hollywood at the dawn of his professional career, few would have imagined that Richard Weitz would become one of the most powerful leaders in the entertainment business. Today, he is cochairman of William Morris Endeavor (WME), the largest talent agency in the world. Weitz reached the pinnacle of his profession by delivering for his clients and building powerful relationships at each step of his journey.

After moving to Los Angeles following his college years and meeting with initial defeat, Weitz finally got his big break. He started working in the mailroom at InterTalent, which later merged with ICM. As he looked over across the desk, he saw Ari Emanuel, current CEO of Endeavor and the man who inspired Jeremy Piven's unforgettable character Ari Gold on the HBO show, *Entourage*. Weitz grinded and found opportunities within each day to learn the business, build relationships, and bring out the best in prospective clients. He became an agent, rising up the ranks to ultimately start the TV department at WME. He surrounded himself with some of the smartest, most successful people in the business. Emanuel helped give him the vision and guidance he needed to continue his progression toward becoming a top Hollywood agent. His main guiding principle was:

I need to learn every day.

Weitz's championship leadership comes from his uncanny ability to see opportunities where others don't. It's his ability to read people and understand how to set them up for success that's helped him to build enduring relationships inside and outside of WME. But it also comes from the experience of learning the industry and having fun. If there's an awards show, event, or client worth meeting, he's there. It's the mindset of opportunity first. Hollywood, like other industries, is about relationships. The assertive, opportunistic leaders rise to the top. Which raises the question, How do you build such powerful, lasting relationships? His guidance here transcends industries and is applicable to all of us.

Weitz told me that *curiosity* is what propels him to do what he does. "If I don't meet five new people per week, I've failed. I'm a straight shooter and I'm looking to find mutually beneficial opportunities. I'm looking to connect; I really want to bring good people together. That's what we do at WME. We absorb opportunities, we see the opportunities to make things happen."[1]

He further details, "You have to give people opportunities and give them the room to grow. You can identify their strengths and weaknesses and encourage them to lean into their strengths. But they need to know it and believe it for themselves."

During the early stages of the COVID pandemic, Weitz sensed the opportunity of a lifetime. As many of us struggled with feeling isolated and disconnected, he recognized he needed to start local and find a way to light up people's lives. Weitz used his connections in the movie, music, and entertainment industries, which he had built over 30 years, to give people the gifts of laughter, joy, and music during a time of loneliness and despair. And the best part about it—he did so in tandem with his daughter, Demi. Together, they launched RWQuarantunes. As he's told me often, "I wouldn't be where I am without my children."

Weitz says RWQuarantunes is what helped him develop an even more special relationship with his daughter, and rediscover the passion of what got him into the entertainment business in the first place. He realized that incredible teams and relationships are formed by trust that becomes friendship.

He was leading people and telling them how to raise money. He brought people together for many remarkable charitable causes such as Make-A-Wish Greater Los Angeles and the Alliance for Children's Rights. He brought the humanity and empathy we all needed back into the social consciousness. And oh yeah—he raised over $38 million for charity. He said, "I have my Co-chair role at WME because of this opportunity (RWQuarantunes)."

The vision of bringing unique personalities together to contribute something magical is a microcosm of the leadership qualities that he's brought to WME. He's helped unite the culture, build camaraderie, and reinvigorate relationships. Weitz is the real deal—out of all the leaders I've worked with, I've never met anyone more authentic and true to who they are. His story is one of someone maximizing their natural abilities and seeing the opportunity in every moment. His candor and authenticity are what inspire relationships—and why it became clear to Endeavor leadership that he was the right person to colead the agency into a new era.

Every time that he speaks to someone, he's thinking of how he'd want to treat that person in a special way. After all, this is how he treats his family, who he loves so much. When he likes something or believes in someone, he takes the initiative and says that he likes it.

He goes out of his way to recognize people and show appreciation with specificity, which is crucial.

Let people know that you're a fan. Let them know that you care. Those are the hallmarks of champion leaders who build teams—and organizations—on camaraderie.

Five Keys for Maximizing Leadership Connection

As we just learned in Richard Weitz's story, the art of communicating and building camaraderie is unique to each person. Whether you have an outgoing personality or are naturally more shy, you can find ways to connect with people. Some of us thrive in team and group settings, while others are better in one-on-one settings. It's good to know where you excel most so you can set yourself up to deal from a position of strength.

I've developed five keys that get to the heart of creating memorable, emotionally intelligent connections. These will help you to build camaraderie with individuals and throughout your organization.

Personalize Your Message: Speak to the Individual

During my college years, our school president was Mark Gearan, who served as director of the Peace Corps, White House communications director under President Bill Clinton, and later as director of The Institute of Politics at the Harvard Kennedy School. He was a man of great accomplishment and a leader who helped take Hobart and William Smith Colleges (HWS) into a new century with optimism and innovation. What was so remarkable about his leadership was the personal touch he had with each student. While HWS was a small school, there was still a student body of over 1,800 students. Gearan made you feel like he'd known you forever—he had an uncanny knack for remembering names and making you feel special.

On the weekend of my college graduation, he hosted students at his house on campus to say both a hello and a goodbye. When I came in with my parents, he smiled and said hi, telling them about my involvement on campus in a variety of activities. I will never forget that he said, "It seems like everywhere I go on campus, I see Christopher. He's done so many great things."

Part of me was surprised he even knew my name.

My amazement was in observing his attention to detail. He went on to account for the work I did for the radio station and various clubs, and you could tell it was informed and sincere. He had that same attention to detail for each student. Some might say at a smaller institution, the leader should have that level of attention. But my years of experience have proven otherwise. Not every leader is willing to personalize relationships.

Champion leaders get on the ground floor, so to speak, and take the time to get to know people. To hear your name, to have someone value your contributions in that way, it's a memory I hold dear to this day. It's why he is revered at my alma mater and recently came back to lead the school for a second time. It's those social skills of making the connection, building camaraderie, and showing pride in each individual that becomes more than the sum of its parts.

Champion leaders use mnemonics to remember details about someone; they make mental notes about someone's name, their contributions, a shared story, or maybe an association with another experience in their life. This gets harder when you're leading a larger organization or department, but the principles remain the same. You may not get to know each person on an intimate level, but you can reach more people through medium-to-large gatherings such as town halls. You can offer recognition for team efforts to projects and have lunches in a cafeteria setting and invite employees to join you. This gives you the opportunity to ask colleagues what they want. The more feedback that you get, the more you'll be able to personalize your approach in return.

Solicit a diverse array of opinions. You can send confidential surveys, too, for those who are more comfortable with providing feedback in that manner.

What *doesn't* work for building camaraderie?

I've seen some organizations foist certain types of events or social gatherings that aren't inclusive and don't cater to what people want. You can have ping pong tournaments, open coffee bars, and foosball tables, but if that's not what people want, then it won't get you very far. Ask your people what benefits and perks they want, and discover how they want to come together. It really is that simple. Ask what value they feel they can get from interacting with their leadership. And remember, communication begins with listening—the best way to personalize your message is to start by listening and showing you care.

Marc Bitzer is the CEO and chairman of the board of the Whirlpool Corporation. He's found that using personalized videos recorded over his iPhone works well for connecting with his employees.[2] He's able to educate and connect with people doing live streams, and he'll answer questions that come in during the Q&A format. He uses his platform to provide company updates and fill people in on the big picture of what's going on company-wide. It's the Q&A portion where he answers unedited questions that endears him more to employees.

One thing I've found through all of my conversations and work with organizations is that people want to feel acknowledged, appreciated, and recognized. Lead with this as your North Star. From there, craft a unique employee experience for your organization.

Champion leaders are *grassroots* leaders who never forget where they've come from and bring that slice of home into personalizing the connection with each person. Remember the learner's mindset: be curious to get to know people. Try and meet several new people in your organization each week and let them know they're welcome to come stop by and say hi to you.

Presence in the Moment: Listen with Full Presence and Eliminate Distractions

Stop what you're doing and listen! The key to being fully present seems so simple, yet when we're balancing a variety of priorities, it's easy to have our mind in one place and our physical body in another. Champion leaders give people their undivided attention and define time parameters up front.

I'll say this as someone who likes to talk (hey, I do it for a living!): don't be afraid to let someone know that you only have a certain amount of time. It's realistic. It's candid. It helps people prepare an agenda and be concise if they need help with something. Also, try to maximize your listening time and attention on building genuine connection. With so many teams now geographically dispersed, there are tactical matters that can be solved over email. Go back to what is most important strategically (see Chapter 5) and remember to build in natural time to get to know people better. You get to decide what you can commit to. But remember to play the long game of building strong relationships that will endure.

A *Stanford Medicine Magazine* article titled "Are You Listening?" explained the bond that doctors try to strike with patients. Dr. Stephanie Harman, a clinical associate professor of medicine at Stanford University, said, "Learning how to build strong patient relationships is equally as important in medicine as learning technical or procedural skills."[3]

This shows that how we bond is equally as important as the knowledge we have—and it's that bond that's at the heart of leadership. In the same article Dr. Donna Zulman said, "Good communication starts with clinicians really absorbing what patients say—about themselves, their pain, values, challenges, and care goals—and being empathetic."

Put your phone down. Close your laptop. And don't be in such a rush. Remember—we know when someone is really paying attention to us and when they're not. Live in that moment with full presence—be there with that person and experience where they're coming from.

Make Your Passion Their Passion (and Make Their Passion Yours): Let Your Fire Shine Through

A chief financial officer that I coached from a Fortune 500 manufacturing company once told me that he made it a goal to get to know each person's passion or favorite thing and always remembered it and referenced it in conversations. Get to know someone's personal interests, what motivates them, and the things that inspire them to do the work that they do. Make their passion yours. When you're genuinely excited and curious to learn more about what inspires them and fires them up, it strikes a chord of connection.

Some people have a why, and others have their "who," which is often family and loved ones. Some people love to do activities that bring them a level of excitement. As we've seen, each generation of employees is motivated to pursue a variety of interests outside of work. Your curiosity can guide you to form relationships, and then have the mnemonics (that we referenced earlier) to be able to lock in these passionate areas of interest to build stronger relationships. Maybe they have a passion for volunteering to help underprivileged youth in the community and you find an opportunity to join in, yourself.

This can be professional or personal, and sometimes the passion can be the ultimate goal of where someone wants to go. A CEO that I've worked with in athletics administration has regular chats throughout the academic year with his executive staff to understand and support their professional ambitions. Working with thousands of organizations over the years, I can tell you it's always best to have this relationship candor and let your desires be known when you have a leader who genuinely cares.

Some employees come to your organization to work on specific projects. Work with your executives and managers to try to align projects by passion, when possible. This won't always work out, but the more prioritized you are and the better you know your team, the more possible this is.

Clarity: Make Your Messaging Clear—and Ask for It in Return

George Bernard Shaw once famously said, "The single biggest problem with communication is the illusion that it has taken place." Let's start there. We hear a lot in leadership about alignment and "getting people on the same page," which is vital. The need for clarity ensures that the right communication has taken place, and that clear direction is provided. I've found time and again that providing clarity is one of the most important things that a leader can do. Leadership comes back to the ABC's of communication: accuracy, brevity, and clarity. Be direct and to the point, concise, and make sure understanding is reached. This doesn't mean that you're always in the mode of telling someone exactly what to do.

You can provide clarity, while also giving someone plenty of autonomy. Autonomy can both be given and earned. Don't rush to give autonomy where it's not yet merited, but understand that when someone has proven themselves, this can be the most empowering way to allow them to work.

What matters is how this agreement is understood by each person. The key here is acknowledgment—both by you and the person (or group) you're speaking to in each conversation. You won't always have time to send someone a list of priorities, but you need to ensure ownership is established. You need to have both the strategic picture covered and tactical details agreed on.

You can both go big and small—know the modes and methods of how to communicate. To reach a larger audience, connect through video calls, email, recorded video messaging, meetings, and conferences and verbally. When in written form, keep things succinct and neat by using bullet points. When speaking, take a tip from my oldest son's first pediatrician. Every time we asked him a question about our son's well-being, he would always respond first by saying, "Short answer, long answer." He'd give us the concise details, and then provide more context. This is a brilliant way to organize your thoughts and communicate effectively.

Remember the ABC's! Determine "time stamps" for when to get updates and confirmations that messages have been received clearly. You can reinforce this by regularly checking in for larger group conversations with more junior employees to ensure understanding.

In "The Cost of Poor Communications," David Grossman reported that "a survey of 400 companies with 100,000 employees each cited an average loss per company of $62.4 million per year because of inadequate communication to and between employees."[4]

Communicating poorly can end up costing you a lot more than dollars and cents. It can create dysfunctional teams. Clarity creates camaraderie—reaching this acknowledgment and understanding with your employees is critical.

The Unspoken Word: What You Don't Say Is Just as Important as What You Do

Think about the knowledge handed down to you from your parents, teachers, coaches, and leaders early on in your life. You probably find yourself thinking of things such as:

- Make eye contact;
- Smile;
- Have open body language;
- Maintain good posture;
- Use appropriate hand gestures; and
- Use appropriate facial expressions.

We know from experience how much a smile, a head nod, and even a thumbs-up can mean when building team chemistry. There's also scientific evidence behind these unspoken forms of communication.

Social scientist Amy Cuddy proposed the theory that "power poses" have an effect on testosterone and cortisol levels and self-esteem. People who assume open postures may experience an increase in power and authority—thus being able to create a more powerful connection with others.[5]

Dr. Michael L. Platt, author of *The Leader's Brain*, talks about the essentials of things such as eye contact and mirroring: "Two of the most effective methods for connecting with your audience, whether an individual or a group, are making eye contact and mirroring (subtly mimicking the gestures of the other person). Both of these methods lead to synchronized brain waves, which are linked to engagement, learning, and good rapport."[6]

Remember to have self-awareness of your body language. Observe how others smile, make eye contact with you, and receive you in conversation. This may require some changes to how you show up. Be willing to make these changes in an effort to come closer together with your team members.

Questions for reflection:

- What are ways you can remember key details about people that you interact with in an effort to build long-term relationships?
- Do you find you're more confident when communicating to a larger group or in one-on-one settings?
- What forms of nonverbal communication do you use most?
- How do you and your team members benefit from in-person time for connection?

The Heartbeat of Your Organization: Celebrating the Wins

As we defined earlier in this book, culture is the "values, beliefs, synergies, commitment to excellence, and camaraderie that serves as the enduring heartbeat of the organization." The champion leader is always aware of the emotional temperature of the organization. They're close to the conversations, leading by example, and sensing when things need to change or keep moving full speed ahead. They also recognize the importance of sharing in team successes.

On Derek Jeter's Hall of Fame plaque in Cooperstown the first line reads, "Heartbeat of a Yankees dynasty." You don't need to know much about baseball to recognize how much the former New York Yankees shortstop meant to North America's most successful sports franchise. For nearly 20 years, Jeter was at the epicenter of every great Yankees achievement—and even some low points. Perhaps what we remember most about his illustrious career are the images of him, arms thrust skyward, celebrating a division title or world championship. It's a reminder of the importance of celebrating our team's wins.

Celebrating wins and sharing in team victories help empower the camaraderie of a culture. And yet, people tell me that they're unwilling to celebrate because they're too focused on the process. Before long, if that's the case, you may go your whole career without taking a bow and sharing in the spoils of victory with your team. You'll miss out on the joys of your accomplishments. You'll miss out on game-changing moments that build high-performing teams.

According to Eric Barker in *Time* magazine: "Next time something good happens, stop whatever you are doing, give it a second and appreciate that moment. . . . The happiness researchers call it 'Savoring.'"[7]

I once coached a leader who was only one year removed from being a director, who suddenly found herself in a senior executive position for a federal government agency. She was modest and saw celebrating her successes as boastful. I worked with her and asked her, "What if you started to associate celebrating each success with giving yourself a boost of confidence?" This paradigm shift was all she needed.

She began celebrating each win and felt so much happier inside. Her happiness boosted her self-esteem, energy level, optimism, and confidence. In the years to follow, this mindset shift helped her land a C-level job. All because she was willing to celebrate the climb up each rung of the ladder.

Celebration can be for ourselves. And it can be shared with others. It literally lifts up our emotions to take part in something communal, something shared with other people. Take this from *The How of Happiness* by Sonja Lyubomirsky: "Sharing successes and accomplishments with others has been shown to be associated with elevated pleasant emotions and well-being. So when you or your spouse or cousin or best friend wins an honor, congratulate him or her (and yourself), and celebrate. Try to enjoy the occasion to the fullest. Passing on and rejoicing in good news leads you to relish and soak up the present moment, as well as to foster connections with others."[8]

I don't know about you, but when I haven't stopped to enjoy life's big and small wins, I find myself anxious and unhappy. I start to focus on what I haven't done. It's the classic half-empty mindset that usually doesn't get us anywhere but stuck and frustrated.

Here's the truth that all of us can accept: Not everything that we've touched has turned to gold. And not everything we create and build will. I've done things I'm proud of, but I've also had my failures and mistakes. Maybe you know the same feeling. The difference is, it's one thing to dwell on these things. It's another to look them in the eye, extract what lessons we can from them, and move on.

Knowing that you've achieved something great and having a willingness to celebrate that win should inspire you to lift someone else up. Check that—work by the principle of multiplication.

Lift several other people up. With the social media world at our fingertips, we have no excuse. Be willing to celebrate and take part in the achievements of others! Chances are, you've had someone who made you feel special. Could be a mentor, coach, colleague, or friend. You know how much it means to be honored.

Why not share that feeling with someone else?

The Championship Trio of Connection

There are three things to look for when trying to form a memorable connection with someone (see Figure 6.1).

- The "What";
- The How; and
- Emotional management.

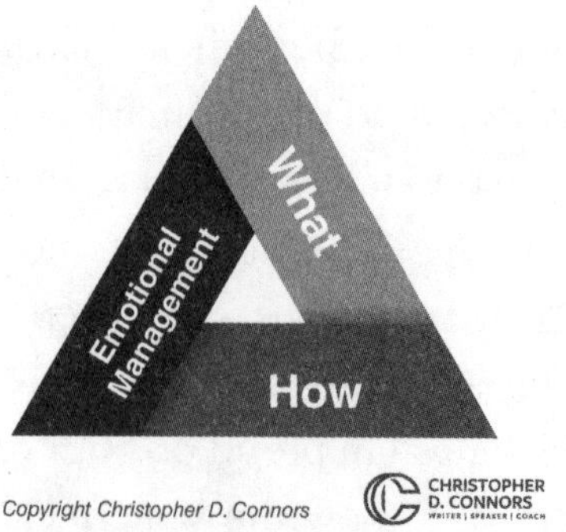

Figure 6.1 The championship trio of connection.
Source: Christopher D. Connors.

The "what" is the message you're delivering. Knowing exactly what you want to say to someone.

The how is about the art and nuance of social skill. It's how you're communicating your "what." This requires knowing your audience and individualizing the way you communicate (both verbal/written word and also body language) to meet someone exactly where they are. For example, you're going to want to provide big-picture details when presenting to a board of directors, whereas you'll need to focus more on tactical details when speaking with early-career employees.

The emotional management is twofold: it's how we show up emotionally, and it's how we want the person we're speaking with to feel. For you, it could mean preparing and building up confidence to show up as authentically as you can. This could mean verbally rehearsing or recording yourself and watching, to see how you're doing, before delivering an employee their annual review. It could also mean managing any fears or anxieties that you have.

From the employee side, we want people to feel valued and respected. When an employee has an issue with one of their colleagues, make it clear that you care about both of them. In this situation, de-escalate the emotions by getting to the facts, listening, and calming people with reassuring words.

The "trio" is an easy-to-remember tool that will prepare you for any conversation.

"He Knew the Names of My Kids": What Gifts Can You Give?

I was flying to speak at a conference in Nashville a couple years ago, right after Herb Kelleher, the cofounder and former CEO of Southwest Airlines, passed away in early 2019. I happened to be flying Southwest Airlines directly from Charleston, South Carolina. As I walked up to the gate to ask a question about the flight, I saw one of the employees greeting people with a big smile. She looked full of vim and vigor. I walked over to her and said hi, and she asked me how I was doing. Given the timing, I decided to ask what her memories were of Herb Kelleher. She paused. I saw her look up with a gleam in her eyes. She wiped a tear away from her eye, looked at me, and said, "D'you know he knew the names of my kids? Always asked me how I was doing—cared for me first as a person. I've worked at Southwest for thirty-five years and got to know him very well early in my time here."

While Southwest certainly used to be a smaller airline, keep in mind it's estimated that they now have over 70,000 employees. I know what you're thinking: How could I memorize all of my employees' names, much less the names of their kids? Spoiler alert—you can't. It's impossible. But it's worth deciding, What is possible? How can you create camaraderie that gives people such a palpable feeling of belonging that many years later it may bring them to tears? Herb Kelleher had a gift. So do you. What uplifting gifts are you willing to give to your employees?

Connecting in Person

After the pandemic, a marketing professional that I coached from a large technology company told me he saw a new light of day. While previously resistant to returning to the office, he discovered how much more effectively he could influence others and develop and promote ideas by collaborating in person. He still loves working from home and appreciates the hybrid balance, as most of us do. It's best for there to be a balance.

For those afforded the luxury to work from home, having time to ourselves to think creatively, and without interruption, is best for the work we do. That said, there is a plethora of firsthand experience from both leaders and employees alike that in-person collaboration leads to greater innovation and getting work done. It produces experiences and team-building moments that can only be achieved when people are co-located. As a leader, it's worth it to reflect on how influential you can be both in-person and virtually. It could shape the future success of your team—and your organization.

As Amazon president and CEO Andy Jassy wrote, "Teams tend to be better connected to one another when they see each other in person more frequently. There is something about being face-to-face with somebody, looking them in the eye, and seeing they're fully immersed in whatever you're discussing that bonds people together. Teams tend to find ways to work through hard and complex tradeoffs faster when they get together and map it out in a room."[9]

Camaraderie and connection form better in-person, but that doesn't mean it's impossible for this to take root in remote environments. It may simply take longer.

According to Microsoft research and analysis, "Overall, we found that the shift to remote work caused the formal business groups and informal communities within Microsoft to become less interconnected and more siloed. Remote work caused the share of collaboration time employees spent with cross-group connections to drop by about 25% of the pre-pandemic level."[10]

One thing I recommend to leaders is to travel quarterly (or at a rhythm that suits you) to visit team members who work from other locations. It's important not to discount the value that can be created with having hybrid schedules, as many companies have implemented this successfully. It's a legitimate challenge every leader faces—knowing there are pros and cons to each.

Disney CEO Bob Iger feels the creative engine of Disney is best served when people are together: "Creativity is the heart and soul of who we are and what we do at Disney. And in a creative business like ours, nothing can replace the ability to connect, observe, and create with peers that comes from being physically together, nor the opportunity to grow professionally by learning from leaders and mentors."[11]

There's opportunity in creating successful teams in both in-person, remote and hybrid environments. Be open-minded, and evaluate this from time to time. Make sure you have the balance that works best for your team.

The Importance of Psychological Safety

Several years ago, Google spearheaded a study to discover the qualities of great teams in their organization. Researchers used 35 different statistical models and reviewed hundreds of variables. They found psychological safety was the top dynamic of effective teams at Google.[12]

Harvard Business School professor Dr. Amy Edmondson defines psychological safety as "a belief that one will not be punished or humiliated for speaking up with ideas, questions, concerns, or mistakes, and that the team is safe for interpersonal risk-taking."[13]

Psychological safety helps to eliminate fear and inspire confidence for employees to speak up to collaborate and work effectively together. Leaders are wise to focus on ways to build the interpersonal relationship first and lead from a place of courage, not fear. This means leading with kindness, getting to know someone, and removing ego from the equation. People can then clearly understand it's about the business, not anything personal.

Great innovations and ideas in business are all about taking risks. If the people on your team are too complacent or hesitant to speak up in fear of retribution, you're going to lose their trust. When trust is lost, you're not innovating, and you're risking far, far more to the future health of your organization.

Psychological safety is showing courage and assertiveness to build relationships and create a team—and culture—that everyone wants to be a part of. It means being proactive in how we communicate! As leaders, if we can agree that communication is a vital soft skill, isn't it better when we're encouraging candid, thoughtful conversations?

It's OK to disagree. It's not OK to criticize and blame others. Set the tone that each voice matters. Establish acceptance and inclusion as cornerstone pieces of a psychologically safe team.

The Spirit of Camaraderie

The mindset change of becoming a leader who fosters camaraderie means processing things through how it might affect your employees *first*. There's a popular acronym that's used in business, called: WIIFM, or what's in it for me? Champion leaders think, "What's in it for *them* (by changing WIIFM to WIIFT). Remind yourself, What was important to you from your manager? Employees want someone who will support them emotionally (well-being), provide them the resources they need, and set them up for success.

Champion leaders are "we" and not "I" leaders. When you view things this way, you're better positioned to help people. On an individual level, you help people to see that their career is not bound by what they're currently capable of doing; it's bound by what they want to do. For the team, you partner with people to create a team identity everyone wants to be a part of. You create opportunities, and share in every success—together. That's the spirit of camaraderie.

Camaraderie Exercise

Focus on removing roadblocks and obstacles for your team. The more as a leader that you can eliminate future burdens and stress, the better. Solicit feedback from each team member on what they see as roadblocks and obstacles. Then, come up with a strategy for how to manage them. This takes strategic thought and listening. It will help you build camaraderie with your team because they'll know you're looking out for them.

Champion's Checklist (Tools and Takeaways)

- ☑ Set the tone in team meetings that it's OK to disagree and challenge one another, as long as it's done respectfully.
- ☑ Reach acknowledgment with team members after each conversation and meeting. If something is unclear, make sure you clarify the details.
- ☑ Prioritize in-person connection time.
- ☑ Eliminate distractions when connecting with your team. Have a "no screen time" rule.
- ☑ Be cognizant of your nonverbal communication and ask, "How would I want to be received?"

Chapter 7

Fortune Favors the Bold Leader (*Learn to Lead with Confidence and Courage*)

"Whatever you can do, or dream you can, begin it. Boldness has genius, power, and magic in it."

—Johann Wolfgang von Goethe

Herb Kelleher refused to play by the rules, for the betterment of a company, an entire industry, and all of us who can profit from his wisdom. Kelleher was the brainchild behind one of the greatest success stories in American business history. He desired to create the best customer experience possible—and by "customer," I mean both the future patrons of Southwest Airlines and his own employees.

When he cofounded Southwest Airlines in the late 1960s, with Rollin King, the vision was clear: make air travel accessible and affordable for millions of people. In his own words, Herb wanted to, "democratize the skies," sure, but he wanted to do it with more panache and spirit than his competitors. That idea started with the customer in mind, but the company's values and mission were built on putting their employees first. Herb Kelleher recognized their worth to the value of Southwest Airlines and championed it throughout his incredibly successful career.

Before a Southwest Airlines plane took flight, Kelleher and his team fought for four long years in legal battles to become operational as an airline. Their first flight was in June 1971.

It was in 1973, less than two years later, that he found himself in a very challenging situation. Southwest's point-to-point model of flying (rather than the conventional hub-and-spoke model in the airline industry) was working well, but he'd found a competitor in Braniff Airlines. Both were competing primarily for business travelers flying routes in the "Texas Triangle" connecting Houston, Dallas, and San Antonio. Braniff Airlines quickly realized Southwest Airlines was a formidable foe and swooped in on their most profitable route (Dallas to Houston). Braniff Airlines cut their prices in half overnight, from $26 to $13.

It was hard to compete with Braniff Airlines' price. Southwest Airlines was charging literally double the fare and needed to in order to stay profitable. So what did Herb Kelleher do? He did what I'd like to believe any rational-minded, business leader would do if put in the same situation.

He decided to offer any person willing to fly Southwest Airlines and pay the full $26 fare a fifth of Chivas Regal scotch.

For that incredible period of time in 1973, Southwest Airlines became the largest distributor of Chivas Regal scotch in the entire state of Texas. A true story!

Kelleher knew he couldn't cut into Braniff Airlines' price, so he decided to get into his customers' hearts. And their liquor cabinets. It led to Southwest's first profitable year. Less than nine years later, Braniff Airlines ceased operations.

So what's the message here? It's obvious, isn't it? Start giving away free premium liquor to your customers! I kid, of course.

The message is that you have permission to be unique, bold, creative, and authentic. You can find a way to connect both with your employees and your customers. In fact, you don't just have permission but a reason to be boldly yourself. This will lead to greater long-term success.

Herb Kelleher was a true original. He drank Wild Turkey bourbon, smoked Kool cigarettes, and showed up to holiday parties dressed like Elvis. He embraced being weird, different, spiritual, and loving. He embraced being himself.

It worked.

He embodied the "Warrior spirit" that he proudly infused into Southwest's culture. Behind the laughs and wisecracks was a brilliant businessman with a sharp, strategic mind who led from the heart. After all, *LUV* is their New York Stock Exchange ticker symbol and they proudly feature a heart on their company logo. Kelleher was always looking to the future and always one step ahead of his competitors. He famously said that a consulting firm approached him and asked to write Southwest's mission statement, and he laughed and said, "By God, if we can't draw up our own mission statement, I think we ought to fold this and go out of business!"[1]

This was someone comfortable in his own skin, who knew his values and understood how to weave them into the fabric of Southwest's culture to achieve mind-boggling success.

Southwest Airlines' remarkable 47-year streak of profitability was no fluke. A great strategy, or a great product can only take you so far. People were flying Southwest Airlines for the ease and price, sure, but they were also flying it for the *experience*. The laughs echoing through the cabin after another joke from a flight attendant. The gracious hospitality. That spirit is a product of bold leadership.

Kelleher inspired change and created one of the best workplace cultures by placing a priceless value on people. He showed that you can lead from the heart and find your own way to reach out and "hug" the people you lead. You can do it directly by finding opportunities to get out and meet people. You can ensure that your message is communicated the same from your lips to your executive team's ears, your organization's middle managers, and front-line employees.

Personalizing your touch, no matter your leadership style, is critical. People will come to know you and your organization through how you treat your people. That's what culture is all about.

By starting local, so to speak, you establish a culture that customers want to be a part of. Your customers come to understand your brand through your culture. People begin to associate a feeling with your organization. People know what they're going to get. A familiar, refreshing, uplifting feeling is what people want—that's the emotion we want to receive when doing business. Let your character and authentic self influence how you lead, and you'll create an unforgettable experience that employees and customers love.

Assertiveness (A Deeper Dive)

Who's up for coffee?

If you want to turn strangers into trusted partners, be outgoing and request "coffee chats" with your peers, direct reports, cross-functional partners, and even senior leaders. If you're not as caffeine-inclined as I am, make it lunch. And pick up the tab!

Being assertive means taking the initiative, even when it's not your nature. The curiosity to learn, grow, and help others can be your guide. Build in time once per week to meet someone for 15 minutes, even virtually. Have a list of things you want to talk about—or just come in looking to get to know someone and ask questions.

A senior director that I've coached told me that she consistently met with her cross-functional peers throughout her first year at the organization. She's more introverted by nature and as a result, more shy and reserved. But she knew she needed to grow as a manager and build relationships to better coordinate work tasks and project success. Despite how awkward it felt at first, she kept going. She pushed past the butterflies. Sometimes she called out the awkwardness to get a laugh from the person she was meeting with!

Her most valuable insight? "I now see the people I work with as humans—and it's made me more empathetic." She built new alliances where they didn't exist before, all because she was willing to take the initiative.

The same thing holds true when looking to resolve an issue, having a challenging conversation, or needing to mediate a discussion between two leaders. Assertiveness asks us to seek the truth—to get to brass tacks and understand what resolution is best for a particular situation. The longer we wait, the more a problem or challenge begins to fester. Emotions are heightened, people begin to dig in their heels, and they draw conclusions and perceptions that often aren't based in fact.

Real talk—we're better off facing and confronting a work problem with assertiveness, integrity, and a genuine desire to help than we are being passive-aggressive or tentative. When people realize we have no ego and only want to bridge a gap or truly help, we gain their trust. When we assume positive intent and seek to create win-win situations, people come on board.

Telling the Truth

As economist Thomas Sowell said, "When you want to help people, you tell them the truth. When you want to help yourself, you tell them what they want to hear."

Boldness and assertiveness requires courage. To be courageous is to tell people the truth—even when it would be more comfortable to avoid a tough conversation. We may start to tense up, get sweaty palms, or get fearful about having a challenging conversation. It's completely normal to feel this way, but don't let it stop you in your tracks. The problem with avoidance—or taking the path of least resistance—is that you can prolong something and make it worse in the long run. Tough conversations—ones that require truth and candor—are harder in the short term, much better in the mid-term, and always the right solution in the long run.

This is why the connection success formula in Chapter 1 matters so much. By being assertive, you're able to hold people accountable, but you can still do so with kindness, courtesy, and respect. Don't let ego get in the way; don't take things too personally. Instill tenets of operation and rules of the road that are informed by practical things, such as "Connecting the CORD" as you'll see in Chapter 8.

Building Relationships

In leadership, communicating with confidence and building relationships that lead to positive results demands the respect of others. To make a well-thought-out decision with authority—that's been vetted and discussed with others—shows you're in control. Relationship building is about taking a chance, and having the gumption and courage to speak up and try.

What I've learned in working with top leaders is, we cannot make assumptions about someone's body language and think they don't want to make time for us. When we get lost in our own heads and develop preconceived notions, we create made-up stories based on our own insecurities. If we really want to get to know someone, we need to persist and persevere to build a relationship.

Your employees won't always tell you how they're feeling and doing. It's possible they've never experienced championship leadership. Sometimes, employees will walk out the door if they feel their work, voice, and opinions aren't valued. It's better to be assertive. This is why prioritizing how you connect with people throughout your organization matters. The more you give out, over time, the more people will come back to you. You won't always have to play offense; you'll create reciprocal lines of communication.

When we boil it down, what's employee engagement, anyway? It's interacting with your colleagues—communicating with them! Literally keeping them engaged by having conversations that come from a desire to educate, inform, and support. Communication begins with listening. Listen to what your team members need; listen to what they want. And find a way to support them. Engagement is a call for the conversation to take place and to know that it's always important to build this time in.

What's retention? Developing a plan to make sure productive, high-performing employees—who make the people around them better—are happy, fulfilled, and set up for future success. Then, they'll want to stay around. You want to keep those people! So give them a reason to stick around beyond pay and title. Ask them for their thoughts on what contributes to crafting an amazing culture. This takes time. It takes adaptability. It takes throwing out some "old ways" in favor of new, modern leadership. You will lessen the likelihood of talented people leaving your organization by connecting more and being there for them.

Assertiveness is about standing up for what you believe in and standing up for the people that you lead. A health care leader that I've coached found herself in the unique position of needing to advocate for a colleague whose reputation had begun to suffer a bit. She knew he was good at what he did and felt it was important to give him an opportunity to succeed. She knew he could work on his emotional intelligence and soft skills and begin to improve them. She was able to see the situation holistically. She had several conversations with him, understood his side of things, and didn't back down from her convictions—even when some senior leaders began to express doubts about him. She saw his current and future potential and recommended him for a leadership role, seeing his skills as translating to higher impact and profit for the organization. Things have worked out. He's learned, grown, and improved. That's what being assertive and championing your employees is all about.

Leadership Is a Contact Sport

Courageous connection means seeing the playing field and determining when, not if, to make a move. Leadership is a contact sport! Connecting with your colleagues is a must. Connection that progresses to meaningful conversations inspires action. We get there by first taking care of ourselves and understanding our motivational drivers. I like to tell my clients, "You're at your best when you're *dealing from a position of strength*." What I mean is, know what mode of connection works best for you and feels most natural. If you feel more comfortable in-person, then over-index on that. If you're sensing that you do better over video, then use that medium, as well. Dealing from a position of strength comes back to leveraging your best interpersonal strengths. It's about showing up confidently and authentically with a desire to positively influence people.

I've coached many introverts who don't enjoy addressing larger groups and often shy away from speaking up in these settings, even when they have great ideas to share. But those same people often thrive in one-on-one settings with colleagues where they can go deep—beyond the superficial. Know where you feel most confident and where you derive your energy from. Focus more of your time there, while working to develop confidence and strength in other settings.

I encourage leaders to send articles or book recommendations to their teams, and to express why they're passionate about it and how it relates to their team's success. Consider this example: When Satya Nadella first took over Microsoft as CEO in 2014, the senior leadership at one of the largest technology companies in the world wasn't communicating with one another. He knew he needed to change the culture. He set up town hall discussions with employees, broadcast webinars on the importance of Microsoft's culture, and held team building sessions with his executives. He didn't just encourage them to talk with one another. He created time specifically for this connection. He gave each leadership team member a book called *Nonviolent Communication*, and had more frequent, high-quality discussions to resolve differences. He asked each person to listen to one another and lead with empathy.

The results were incredible. Microsoft's leaders started speaking with one another again. They put their egos aside and started to have the necessary conversations that have continued to keep Microsoft at the vanguard of technology and as one of the world's most profitable companies.

To be empathetic, you must first be self-aware and confident in who you are. To be courageous in how you build relationships with others, it helps to bring your best each day. This breeds self-confidence that is empowered by the inner work of growing, learning, and knowing yourself better each day.

One of the reasons that sports stories and movies are so motivating is because the protagonists are able to capture precisely how to empower and motivate the athletes who are about to take the field to compete. We've seen it in movies such as *Coach Carter*, *Rudy*, and *The Rookie*. In so many respects, amateur, college, or pro, those athletes *really* want to be there in the arena competing. Coaches may not be able to control whether someone shows up or not, but they have a profoundly powerful ability to influence, cultivate, and motivate someone's desire when they *do* show up.

Like a sports coach, you don't control someone's ability to show up for work and carry out the basic responsibilities of their job. But you sure have the ability to motivate, empower, and provide your team with the tools and skills to perform their job at a high level. You can show—and tell—them how to show up and give the very best that they have each day. This is accomplished by clearly defining roles, responsibilities, purpose, mission, and goals. It's also heavily influenced by the way you show up each day with your own desire to be great. It's the consistency of this leadership by example that inspires dedication, and commitment to executing at a high level that leads to the formation of a high-performing team.

Put your own stamp on it, while allowing your team members to put theirs. The more you go all-in, the more they will go all-in if they know that you care about them—and if they know that you will truly be there to help them when they need it.

Playing Offense and Defense

I talk a lot with clients about what it means to play offense and defense in leadership. Playing offense means taking every positive action that you can to influence a given situation. Playing defense means that you limit or eliminate the turnovers and prevent negative things from happening.

Let's look at how you can play offense as a leader:

- Set up a one-on-one with a direct report, peer, or colleague you haven't gotten to know yet.
- Carve in time for 30 minutes, every other week, to make notes and reflect on career progress and development actions for team members.
- Have a call or a quick in-person greeting if you need to "clear the air" on something with a colleague. This shows humility and a "No hard feelings" approach that goes a long way.

- Highlight a contribution to the *process* (not just a result) that someone made and recognize that person in the appropriate forum.
- Drop by one new business unit each week to observe, be curious, and learn more about a process, product, or technology you're not familiar with.

Now, let's see how you can play defense as a leader:

- Apply self-care principles such as taking a needed day off to rest and recharge.
- Step away for a few minutes to collect yourself, particularly during or following a challenging discussion or moment.
- Know what to say no to. This means determining strategies that could be good but not great. It means evaluating opportunities to see what is in the best interest of your organization. And it means deciding where you're best suited to spend your time each week. Take this powerful insight on solitude from Mike Erwin: "Solitude gives you the space to reflect on where your time is best spent, which provides you with the clarity to decide which meetings you should stop attending, which committees you should step down from, and which invitations you should politely decline."[2]
- Call out *what* is not working. Focus your energy on crafting the *how* part of communications to ensure you're not hurting or harming anyone but, instead bringing them along with you.
- Create a risk assessment to anticipate the biggest potential negative impacts and to figure out how to mitigate these and create responsiveness toward them.

Questions for reflection:

- What's one way you can lead more boldly for your team?
- How can you use both candor and kindness in telling your team that something isn't working—and that it's time to try something different?
- What have you learned from bold leaders that you most admire and want to assimilate into your own style of leadership?
- What have you learned from leaders that you didn't respect or admire that has informed you of what you don't want to do?

Live Boldly

Living boldly means confidently carrying out the plans you set out to accomplish. What you think, say, and do all stem from your confidence. This mindset believes that thoughts, words, and actions will lead to a life of helping others feel fulfilled, as well as finding the same fulfillment for yourself. Living boldly is about speaking positive, empowering words over your life and inspiring yourself and the people around you. It means you accept every challenge as an opportunity to improve and grow stronger. This leads to confidence and self-assurance.

When you live boldly—with confidence—life begins to come to you naturally, clearly, and freely. You stop worrying and start living. You achieve a life in harmony and rhythm, one where you exude confidence. Living boldly means living with an open mind and open heart. It requires keen self-awareness, self-control, and an insatiable desire for achieving success.

The mantra of *live boldly* means being a deep thinker and doer who works earnestly to add value to the lives of others. It means believing in people with maximum faith. Belief is about inspiring clear communication, promoting confidence, and ensuring that conversations take place at every layer of your organization from top to bottom. Over-communicate. If the worst they can say about you is that you occasionally repeat your messaging, then you're doing pretty well.

The Power of Reinvention

Do you believe in the power of reinvention? In life, in leadership, the opportunity is always there for us to be who we truly want to be for others. It's the central theme of one of my favorite movies, *Groundhog Day*. As Bill Murray's character in the film, Phil Connors (no relation!), hilariously shows us, we can go about doing things the wrong way, we can get cynical, become discouraged, and go through the motions in life (and our jobs). But where does that really get us?

Right back to where we started in most instances.

And for Phil Connors, it was repeating the same day over and over again. See the parallels? It isn't until we act with positive intentions—the genuine desire to help, serve, and lift others up—that we can become transformational as leaders. It's about the ability to reinvent ourselves and behave in a way that ties to our values and is the way we'd want others to treat us. This brings out creativity, professionalism, and energy. The irony of Phil Connors' quest in *Groundhog Day* was that he simply needed to do the right things to unlock the life he really wanted.

The same goes for leadership. I've worked with thousands of organizations throughout my career. No one truly wants to treat others poorly or play in a zero-sum game. And yet, with poor leadership, it's easy to see why many people feel that way and ultimately leave an organization. So I throw down the gauntlet to you.

There's always the opportunity to reinvent yourself. This requires boldness. There's always an opportunity to learn, grow, and be the leader for others that you'd want someone to be for you. It takes work. It takes a desire to change and the will to be transformative as a modern leader. But it is possible. And it's rooted in self-awareness, empathy, and a genuine desire to let people know you care about them.

The Reinvention of a Titan

In 1985, less than 10 years after he founded Apple, Steve Jobs was (effectively) fired.

Only 30 years old, he needed to move on from the only business he'd ever known. Jobs was forced to resign when CEO John Sculley felt Apple needed to reorganize and shift gears. He didn't see Jobs in the tech company's future plans. So he was let go.

It would take nearly 12 years before Jobs came back to the company that he started. During his time away from Apple, Jobs founded NeXT, a company that developed computer workstations. He also provided funding for Pixar and helped the animation studio to get off the ground and grow. He later became chairman and was an executive producer on the enormous hit movie *Toy Story*. During his time away, Jobs reinvented himself and used his talents to grow two other organizations.

Once Jobs returned in 1997, he guided Apple into a new frontier of technological advancement and success. Products such as the iPod, iPad, and iPhone would come to define the way we all use technology—in the palms of our hands.

And yet, one of the best lessons we can learn from Jobs's life is the same one he learned during his nearly 12-year hiatus from Apple.

As he said: "I didn't see it then, but it turned out that getting fired from Apple was the best thing that could have ever happened to me."[3]

The man we remember as one of the most successful CEOs and leaders in business history profited most from an incredible, embarrassing failure. This failure influenced the way he thought and how he would innovate and use technology as his tool to change the way billions of people live.

He came back better than ever because he knew he wanted to create game-changing products that people didn't yet know they wanted—and needed. Steve Jobs loved what he did. He said: "Your work is going to fill a large part of your life, and the only way to be truly satisfied is to do what you believe is great work. And the only way to do great work is to love what you do. If you haven't found it yet, keep looking. Don't settle. As with all matters of the heart, you'll know when you find it."[4]

Jobs ultimately became a very wealthy and successful man because he was forced to do some introspection and determine how he could get better. He never stopped innovating—this time, he took the opportunity to grow both professionally and personally.

He mended some of the personal relationships in his life, both with his previous partner and children. He later remarried during his time away from Apple and continued his evolution into becoming a more well-rounded man.

He kept searching, kept looking, and made personal growth a lifelong quest. Jobs could have let getting fired from Apple define him for the rest of his life in a *bad way*. Instead, he used that moment as an opportunity to reinvent himself and converted it into an exemplary model of growth. This is Jobs's greatest lesson, and one we can all heed in our own lives.

A Few Important Lessons

A big part of being bold is a willingness to stare down failure and trust your gut. Refer back to the priceless lessons and wisdom you've gained from the times you've fallen short. Success comes in the way we see ourselves, how we own up to our shortcomings, and how we choose to make ourselves and the people around us better.

There's a lot to learn from the boldness of Steve Jobs on both sides of the coin—that persevering and believing in yourself is what separates great achievers from the rest. You can have it all—you can do this by caring for people and holding them to a high standard, while still looking out for their needs and treating them with kindness and respect.

The other side of the coin is that Steve Jobs burned some bridges and didn't always put the needs of others first. He was a visionary leader who placed a huge premium on product excellence. Sometimes, that harmed relationships in the process. He pushed some employees to their limits—and some out the door. His ascent to the top of the technology and leadership world wasn't perfect.

To be clear—I don't condone the way he behaved, at times. However, there's a reason we'll be studying his leadership style, legacy, and success at Apple for generations to come. Part of being a champion leader means discerning what is right and wrong. Take the positives that you can take from studying other leaders, and assimilate those qualities into your leadership style. The negatives? You can leave those in your wake. It's equally as important to know what we don't want to do and learn from the attributes of bad leadership. Put those things in the garbage disposal, where they belong.

Jobs had both passion and vision. He refused to accept second best, and he refused to be denied in crafting the creative vision he believed in. He never settled. He worked each day with a subject matter that he cared about, which made it that much easier to talk about, market, and sell.

His indomitable will to innovate and cast a vision to create a brighter future is to be admired. Another lesson we can take from Steve Jobs's leadership is to never compromise on holding yourself and others to a higher standard. As a champion leader, you can do this with kindness, empathy, and respect for others.

Be Willing to Give Boldness a Shot

You have more time than you think to build the career you want and leave an incredible impact on others. When I speak to organizations at conferences and meetings, I'm often asked in the Q&A portion at the end to give advice. I always say, "Live with an optimistic outlook, treat others with kindness and respect, and find the opportunities in all that you do."

Always maintain a positive outlook. If you're willing to learn from your failures, you will see a brighter day. Never ever take any experience for granted. Learn from every experience. Be truly grateful for the opportunities you have. The tough times make us mentally and emotionally resilient. This is what leads to a growth mindset and sets the pace for the goals we aim to achieve throughout our lives.

If you're wondering whether you should send that email you've been thinking about sending for a business opportunity—send it. If you've been on the fence about reaching out to a colleague with a great idea for their career development—don't hesitate, reach out. That could be the coffee chat you set up this week. Be kind. Be generous with your time when it comes to helping someone else. And remember the famous Latin proverb: *audentes fortuna juvat*—fortune favors the bold.

Fortune Favors the Bold Leader Exercise

I call this "bold truths and humble admissions." Think about one bold truth and one humble admission that you can share in one-on-one conversations with team members and cross-functional partners. Think of this as an icebreaker that comes from a place of care. Boldness brings us closer together in relationships. Always take the lead. Share one bold truth about yourself and one humble admission of a mistake, failure, or fun idiosyncrasy about you. As always, you can share both personal and professional stories. Be bold! Initiate the conversation, and your employees will follow your lead.

Champion's Checklist (Tools and Takeaways)

☑ Approach each conversation with confidence—lead with positive intent.

☑ Be weird. Be different. Laugh about being weird and different. Be yourself.

☑ Remember that it's just as important to limit bad mistakes (play defense) as it is to produce successful outcomes (play offense).

☑ Always tell people the truth. Champion leaders are compassionately honest.

☑ Recognize your team members' contributions to both the process and end results with equal exuberance and praise.

Chapter 8

Connecting the "CORD" (*Communicate, Identify Opportunities, Build Relationships, and Make Smart Decisions*)

"Customizing your approach creates connection with people that enables them to give the best of what they have. This is about maximizing performance, trust and rapport."

—Jeffrey Hirsch

STARZ President and CEO Jeffrey Hirsch knows a lot about turning connection into an art form—it's part of what's led him to the forefront of innovation and success in the entertainment industry. Hirsch started his career ascending the executive ranks at Time Warner Cable and then landed at STARZ in 2015. He earned the opportunity to lead the television network, proving himself in several executive roles before ultimately becoming president and CEO in 2019, at a time of significant disruption in the industry.

Along his journey, he learned that self-awareness and adaptability would help guide how he communicates, identifies opportunities, builds relationships, and makes smart decisions. It takes a bold understanding of ourselves and a willingness to understand others. As he told me, "It's easier for you to adjust yourself to each individual rather than them trying to adjust themselves to you."[1] This emotionally intelligent approach is rooted in the leadership lessons he's learned along the way, which are summarized in the following quote:

> *If you hire good people who care about the mission of your business, and you commit to building connections with them and keeping them engaged and focused on the mission, you're going to have a great culture.*

Hirsch saw his charge as STARZ president and CEO to re-create the brand as one that serves women, one of its core audiences. He started by hiring more women to surround himself with talented female voices, and now the majority of the executive leadership team are women, most of whom are women of color. He built a diverse and inclusive network of decision makers whose ideas have connected with viewers.

What's separated him as a leader has been his willingness to listen, understand, and adapt to what viewers and customers want most. He's put the right people in positions to be successful and gives them the latitude to play to their strengths.

Hirsch emphasized the need to develop programming that appeals to a more diverse audience. STARZ has fostered and supported television series that lift up the voices of women and underrepresented communities. They've done extensive research to learn what their audience is most interested in so they can optimize both the content and the way it is presented.

In a 2022 interview with McKinsey, Hirsch said, "We saw five years ago what was actually driving our business, and that was underrepresented audiences and voices. . . . And we turned that insight into a kind of programming mandate: we are going to put stories on the air that are by, for, and about women and underrepresented audiences."[2]

I was smart enough to realize he was willing . . . and he was smart enough to realize I wanted.

Hirsch recognized early in his career, through an influential professional mentor, that he was attracted to people-first leadership. He moved away from his northeast roots and headed south to Columbia, South Carolina, where he learned the ropes from a senior leader who showed a deep care and concern for people. Hirsch admired the way this man treated everyone—and how he individualized the way he communicated to each person. He realized leadership success is a balance of business strategy, execution, and empathy for your employees.

He told me, "It's connecting with people all throughout the organization and being able to simplify how you communicate to help people understand strategy and how to execute. You need to understand the nuance of how to relate with people."

As we've seen in the stories of other leaders, the secret to Hirsch's success has been prioritizing results, adapting to the needs of his customers and employees, and making time to show that he cares. There's one other key ingredient that really matters: simplicity. As he told me: "If you keep things simple, things will work. When you make things complicated, you lose."

Knowing your audience is an adage for leaders in every industry—it helps you calibrate the way you connect. Communicating and building relationships that serve customers requires listening to the voice of the customer. The same can be said for your employees. Hirsch has excelled in both areas at STARZ—and it's made the difference in how the network is connecting with everyone worldwide.

Connecting the CORD, as you'll find out in this chapter, is a way for you to keep top of mind the importance of building connection, staying nimble as a leader, and focusing on opportunities and key decisions as they come up. (See Figure 8.1.)

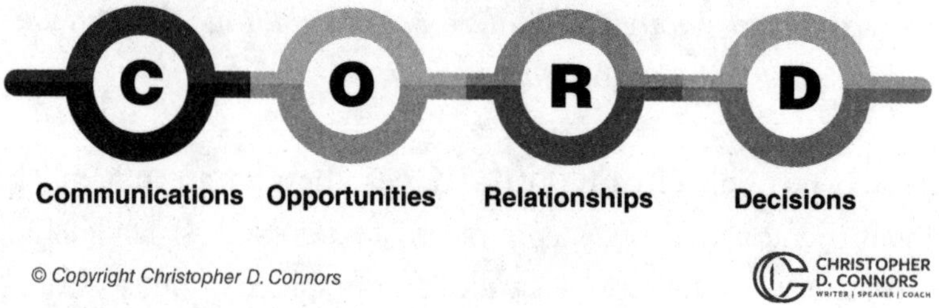

Figure 8.1 Connecting the CORD.
Source: Christopher D. Connors.

Communication

> *"Whether it's oral communications or written communications, if you cannot simplify a message and communicate it compellingly, believe me you cannot get the masters to follow you."*
>
> —Indra Nooyi[3]

Big, arcane words aren't helpful when it comes to bringing people together. As we learned from Jeffrey Hirsch, it's wise for leaders to simplify their message. This comes back to needing to be clear in how we communicate because without simple direction, people cannot move forward. Start here: every time you need to communicate direction, think about how you'd need to tell it to a kindergartner. Even with three young boys at home, this can still be challenging for me! It's a reminder that the best leaders simplify difficult concepts by breaking them into bite-sized chunks.

Daniel Kahneman writes in *Thinking Fast and Slow*, "If you care about being thought credible and intelligent, do not use complex language where simpler language will do."[4] Great processes are pieced together with simple communication. Make it easy to understand, and chances are you'll have team members who are clear the first time around.

Having the Tough Conversations

One of the most common, challenging conversations is delivering someone a negative or poor review during the annual performance review process. Let's face it—no one ever wants to do it. Many employees don't realize how much leaders dread these conversations. It's nerve-racking, and we all fear being disliked, to some degree, by our colleagues. It feels terrible to have to tell someone they're fired; they're not getting a pay raise; they performed below expectations; they're being put on documented coaching or a performance improvement plan. But, to be a champion leader is to work closely with someone and support their development and improvement for every day they work at your organization. There should never be surprises, which means having a consistent communications cadence.

Don't avoid these conversations. Instead, see how they benefit everyone in the long run.

A C-level executive that I've coached from a leading insurance company told me he learned early on in his career to always approach tough conversations with authenticity and sincerity. You build trust through authentic, personal connection that precedes the professional conversations. Make the person you're speaking with feel at ease. If they're nervous, agitated, or afraid, they're going to have a much harder time taking the news. And you'll naturally be less effective at delivering it. While you can't control how someone reacts, you're best suited to show up as confidently and authentically as you can. In other words—the worst mistake is trying to be someone that you think you should be, when all you need is to be yourself.

Author Nancy Duarte writes in *Resonate*, "If you really believe in what you're communicating, speak confidently about it and don't back down. It's scary to be ridiculed or rejected, but sometimes that's the price."[5]

Communicate with the values of honesty, openness, integrity, and respect, and maintain the professional relationship, while also showing you're an advocate for that person. Showing up with confidence is as much about mindset as it is about preparation. I find the best tool for improving our mindset is to know we're delivering the truth and helping someone in the long run.

While it hurts to receive tough news, you'll gain the long-term respect of someone who understands that you have their best interest in mind. The truth must be the unifying thread that helps you to see past the difficulty of having the initial conversation.

I encourage leaders preparing to have challenging conversations to write an outline of what they want to say in advance. A term used frequently by the US military—bottom-line up front or BLUF—helps us to prioritize the most important, succinct details first. Then, we can provide more details from there.

It's wise to build in time for listening and to allow someone to express themselves. Verbally rehearse yourself speaking in "mumbles" at a monotone pace, and then practice with voice inflection, tone, and the emotions needed to match the magnitude of the situation. It's always best for empathy to shine through in how you communicate and connect with someone.

Duarte says again in *Resonate*, "You need to defer to your audience because if they don't engage and believe in your message, you are the one who loses. Without their help, your idea will fail."

Remember that avoidance is always going to be worse and might prolong negative emotions such as fear, stress, or anxiety for both leaders and colleagues. Avoidance also tends to prolong an awkwardness when people don't yet know each other and as a result, don't feel comfortable speaking with one another.

Where the champion leader shines is in bridging relationship gaps and connecting with a shared interest or commonality to help spark initial conversation. Let's face it—getting to know someone at first can be awkward. But when you can lead without ego, no matter how accomplished you are, and see the relationship as benefiting you, the other person, and the team, you'll lead more authentically. Let that person give their account, listen, and then give yours. Find the common ground and move forward with confidence.

Managing Up

Regardless of your level in the organization, managing up is an integral part of every champion leader's job. Knowing what it means to manage up is also one of the most commonly asked questions I get. Contrary to some popular definitions, I don't see managing up exclusively as making your boss's job easier, although that's certainly part of it. There's no such a thing as managing up in a nutshell. It's multifaceted. Here's a better breakdown of what constitutes managing up:

- Keeping leadership informed of work progress both tactically and strategically;
- Asking for feedback and coming for help after you've presented a solution;
- Learning more about your manager/leader's communication and leadership style;
- Collaboration on strategic decision-making;
- Having a crystal clear understanding of your manager/leader's top priorities, interests, and areas they're most wanting to explore as opportunities;
- Owning the agenda and proactively championing your own development;
- Advocating on behalf of your team's development and results; and
- Understanding that *how* you're telling the story is paramount to getting what you want.

Julie Zhuo, cofounder of Sundial, says, "Make sure you and your manager have the same answers to these two key questions: (1) What is success for me personally? (2) What is success for my manager's team? If you aren't sure your manager knows what you care about, or you don't know what your manager cares about, ask in your next one-on-one."[6]

It's in these one-on-ones where the real opportunities to manage up occur. This is where you ask to own parts of the agenda and contribute thoughts that help to bridge the connection between the two of you.

Julia Banks, Director of Global HR Operations at Zendrive, says, "With observation over time, you can learn how your leader processes inputs. For example, one of my bosses had a tendency to stop listening after my first sentence, because his mind would race to find solutions. . . . Once I observed this, I flipped the order of my words, which made a huge difference in our relationship. Instead of saying, 'Here is the problem, and here's what I propose we do,' I would say, 'Here is what I propose we do to solve this problem.'"[7]

In his book *Theodore Roosevelt on Leadership: Executive Lessons from the Great Communicator*, James Strock highlights how President Roosevelt was a proponent of always communicating vision to all members of the organization. It's this continual approach of over-communicating that makes leaders successful. "A vital element of Roosevelt's success as an executive was his constant communication of his vision. His uncanny ability to identify with his audiences included the members of the organizations he led. In each of his management positions he enunciated a visionary action agenda."[8]

Keep things simple and clear. Prepare, and you'll feel more confident. Connect, and everyone will be aligned.

Opportunities

Over 25 years ago while in high school, I was attending one of the most prestigious basketball camps in the country, Five-Star Basketball Camp, outside of Pittsburgh. I was mesmerized by this counselor who was a dribbling wizard and great instructor of the game. So I made a point to remember the name, Tobin Anderson, and figured, Who knows where his basketball life will lead him—or where mine will lead me?

When I made it to Hobart and William Smith Colleges and played for the men's basketball team, there he was, coaching Clarkson University with the same intensity he would later bring to Fairleigh Dickinson University's epic March Madness run in 2023. Trying to beat us, trying to win the right way with passion, grit, and fundamentals.

When I started coaching boys' varsity high school basketball in northern Virginia while working full-time in the consulting world, he was one of the first coaches I reached out to for advice. He wrote me back and congratulated me on the coaching job. He sent me a DVD and some practice drills to use with the team. Most significantly, he told me to believe in myself, never stop working hard, and see the opportunity in each day. They're words I've never forgotten.

One thing I've learned is success comes in all shapes, sizes, and times for everyone. You never know when your big opportunity or break will come. You have to believe, be ready, and work hard. As I reflect on Coach Anderson's remarkable 2023 NCAA Tournament run with Fairleigh Dickinson—and his great coaching career—I see a lifer, someone who has worked for everything he's had. And now, everyone is getting to see his energy, passion, and desire.

Hopefully, many more will see what class, grace, and a willingness to help someone looks like. The information he sent me at the beginning of my high school coaching career helped me a lot. It gave me hope. It stoked a fire inside of me that propelled me forward in other areas of my career.

You never know when your incredible opportunities will come. Coach Anderson grinded for years at the Division 3 and 2 levels, and now, he's getting the opportunity to compete with the best teams in the country in Division 1. His dedication and opportunistic approach made him one of the top basketball coaches in the country. It's how you take advantage of the opportunities given to you that matters in becoming a champion leader.

Put Yourself in a Position to Be Helped

The other side of helping is putting yourself in a position to be helped! Might sound simple, but this is a critical nuance to master. How do you do it?

- Be a great listener.
- Check your ego at the door.
- Ask for feedback, and when you receive it, ask follow-up questions and discern what actions you can take.
- Be open-minded; see any piece of information as an opportunity or nugget worth evaluating/analyzing.

Additionally, while it's common for those of us who hold ourselves to a high standard to sometimes be shy or deflecting of praise and recognition, I encourage you to accept praise with gratitude. Let it educate, inform, and build your confidence. This prepares you for the next opportunity! Don't be afraid to tell your leadership what you need to be successful. It takes courage to speak up and an opportunistic mindset to know what to say.

Learners See Opportunities

As Matt Damon says in the movie *Rounders*, "You can't lose what you don't put in the middle. But you can't win much either."[9]

You need to decide how to boldly risk professionally, and do things that are in alignment with your values, while also giving yourself stretch opportunities to innovate and do greater than you ever imagined. Champion leaders go above and beyond and don't just play it safe. They have a learner's mindset and are willing to make the extra effort. Humble leaders with a learner's mindset are the most successful ones I know.

To be a great learner, you have to give it a shot. You must be self-aware and willing to learn from your mistakes. Sometimes, you're going to succeed on the first go. Sometimes, you're going to fail, make a mistake, or not connect.

Here are the benefits from experiential learning, which means putting yourself in a position to positively influence others at each step:

- You get to *engage* the people you lead, learn more about them, find out what makes them tick, and build thriving relationships.
- You *reflect* on business strategies that haven't worked, those that have, and how to eliminate future mistakes.
- You learn from *listening* to your team members about what they want for their career development, their strategic ideas, and what they want the culture of your company to continue to evolve into being.

Remember—not every touchpoint, decision, or action will always be a rousing success. But as T.S. Eliot famously said, "Only those who will risk going too far can possibly find out how far one can go." Be willing to go the extra mile. Be willing to give everything you have to make your organization successful. Be willing to make a mistake or two. You'll learn. You'll grow. And everyone will be better for it.

> Questions for reflection:
>
> - Think of a strategic message that you're planning to deliver to your team; how could you simplify the wording to ensure better understanding?
> - What's the most valuable leadership lesson you've learned in your career?
> - How well are you building relationships with employees in the field?
> - What criteria matter most to you when evaluating how to make a decision?

Balancing Our Leadership

There's a magic that is revealed when building high-performing teams—sometimes the greatest ideas come together when shared. Other times, the most powerful innovations come from allowing people the space to be themselves and do great work.

Author Susan Cain explains the value of affording employees the opportunities to both connect and be very much their own, independent selves to drive results. She shares the story of Apple cofounder, Steve Wozniak:

> Before Mr. Wozniak started Apple, he designed calculators at Hewlett-Packard, a job he loved partly because HP made it easy to chat with his colleagues. Every day at 10 a.m. and 2 p.m., management wheeled in doughnuts and

> coffee, and people could socialize and swap ideas. What distinguished these interactions was how low-key they were. For Mr. Wozniak, collaboration meant the ability to share a doughnut and a brainwave with his laid-back, poorly dressed colleagues—who minded not a whit when he disappeared into his cubicle to get the real work done.[10]

Understanding the balance of collaboration and independent time as a leader allows people to do their best work and come in refreshed for each new opportunity.

Development Goals and Actions

The development goals or actions that come from annual reviews and one-on-one conversations should never be viewed as daunting. See them as growth opportunities that are able to foster a feeling of optimism and belief. When you can point to specifics as to why you feel past performance will carry over to strong, future performance, you've drawn a foundational purpose that can carry you forward. The language we use also matters. Use opportunistic, encouraging language when working with employees on their development actions.

Robert Cialdini writes in *Pre-suasion*, "Multiple studies have shown that subtly exposing individuals to words that connote achievement (win, attain, succeed, master) increases their performance on an assigned task and more than doubles their willingness to keep working on it."[11]

I think about a challenge that faces leaders in every organization: trying to project the future performance of individual contributors and how their successes can translate over to managing people. When we really think about it, putting someone in the capacity to lead others—when they've never actually done so—is a gamble. It shows faith and optimism in a person that they will succeed. When it works right, this is precisely the belief that leads to growth opportunities for an individual and growth for an organization. It's why every organization needs to evaluate employees, understand what they want, and get frequent feedback through formal surveys and manager conversations. When someone leaves an organization, it's in part a reflection that they didn't get what they wanted and perhaps worse—what they needed.

The underpinning of success is desire. We're innately wired to connect. We want to help others grow and succeed together. Find the people in your organization who have this burning desire, and you'll increase the probability of planting the seeds for future champion leaders. Be willing to give people the opportunity to lead.

Relationships

Relationships are at the core of everything we do. The way we support our clients, the way we make deals, and how we have fun in the process all tie back to relationships. People come first. You flourish because of your relationships. This is perhaps the chief unifying thread in champion leaders I've coached. Organizational success depends upon people. Results depend upon people! It's why respect must be driven home in messaging and actions. It means proactively communicating and having the mindset to always look out for one another and our clients.

Remember to have fun along the way. I tell clients, don't forget to have fun! No matter how high you climb, remember where you came from and why you're in the role you're in. Leaders need to get back to their roots. Remember the purpose of why you're here and the drive you can cultivate in everyone to work together and be the best.

Get Out There

Earlier in my career, I helped lead the oversight and management of an enterprise program management office for a major New York

City government agency. In a large organization, communicating in a timely manner was essential. As we entered into a new era of technology and communications, it was easy at times to get complacent. I remember telling my department leader that I was having difficulty reaching people and wasn't getting responses over instant messenger or email. What followed were words that gave me the jolt I needed to act. He said, "Get off your butt and go to their office and ask them!"

It's one of the most important messages I ever received about effective communication. When a face-to-face conversation is required, waste no time. Get off your butt, and make it happen.

Champion leaders are courageous and know that sitting behind a desk won't help for long. As Indra Nooyi, former CEO of Pepsi, said, "As a leader, you should be out in the field all the time with your customers, with your marketplace, with your channels, with your salesmen, with your manufacturing people. You're going to accomplish nothing sitting in the office . . . get the hell out. Walk, walk the market, meet the customers, meet people who make a difference to the business."[12]

When coming into a new role or a new organization, focus on building relationships first. You want to identify allies and "rocks" who will contribute ideas, and buy into your vision and strategic goals. Start by finding your champions and understand who you can trust and influence. This takes getting out there and having conversations, and applies to exactly where you are as a leader in your respective field. We want the lieutenants and delegates who are our rocks and champions to be force multipliers that bring optimism, energy, and passion to employees at all levels of our organization.

Setting Expectations

Communicating data with metaphors and easy-to-understand real-world examples requires you to know your audience and think of commonly accepted practices. Things such as establishing and setting expectations. Some people like to call it "rules of the road"; I like to refer to this as the communication tenets of operation that every organization and team can establish. For meetings, you can break it down this way:

- Status report/updates: They provide program, project, or task updates on key initiatives.
- Innovation/brainstorming: Often overlooked, having built-in time for each team member to discuss ideas and brainstorm together contributes to new, more efficient ways of doing business, new strategies, and solving problems.
- Decision-making: Determine the chief decision maker for each situation.
- Team building: Define goals and objectives—and don't forget to have fun.
- Compliance: Make sure that everyone abides by organizational policies, laws, and regulations—with no exceptions.
- One-on-one or team meetings: Set an agenda, and always allow room for questions.
- Announcement/information: Choose the communication channel, and let people know there is important news that will affect them.

Provide a clear understanding for what constitutes a(n)

- In-person team meeting or a one-on-one meeting;
- Virtual video conversation;
- Phone call;

- Email; and
- Instant messaging conversation.

This also helps to shape the identity of your organization or team, which we'll talk more about in Chapter 11. You want to create easy-to-follow processes that become habits and are ingrained in the way everyone operates so they don't have to think about it. Reducing the cognitive load of your team frees up their creative thinking ability and reduces redundancies and stress. For each team member to function at their best, understanding what constitutes each mode of communication and knowing exactly what types of meetings should be scheduled will help align everyone. Having these tenets of operation on a team site creates shared visibility.

Building Relationships That Lead to Innovation

By building connected relationships with your team members, you're creating future opportunities for collaboration and innovation. Motivation builds inspiration, and yes, motivation can and should be a discipline. This matters for building a great culture, sure. But it matters equally as much for executing a business strategy and driving results.

Connected relationships bring people together to achieve a mission. When you're motivated behind purpose, goals, and a desire to build an esprit de corps in your culture, you are laying the groundwork for success, which leads to innovation, optimism, and collective grit that can ignite the spirit of an entire organization. Psychologist and Professor Amy Cuddy said, "Before people decide what they think of your message, they decide what they think of you."[13]

Think about that for a second.

Before strategy, before vision, before goals, before any of that, people are forming conscious and subconscious thoughts of who you are and whether they want to embrace your leadership. Having top-down organizational leadership over someone guarantees very little. If you don't work to build and enhance this relationship each day, you run the risk of losing it.

Start by asking each person about the things they enjoy most during their free time and what their passions and hobbies are. Then, you can begin to ask how you can help them. You can also give it a shot based on what you've learned. Ask them about their family. Ask about their professional ambitions. Get to the core of the things they're passionate about personally and the things that drive them professionally.

This is how you begin to personalize the relationship. This is how you motivate others, and in turn it brings it back to self-motivation for you. It leads to a very important question: What impact are you having in building relationships with your team?

Types of Leaders

You've learned about what makes someone a champion leader. It's worthwhile to point out other kind of leaders, as well. Here's a breakdown of what I've observed in many organizations.

Champion leader: A leader who focuses on business results, transformation, new ideas, and each employee's growth, development, and well-being; organized, prioritized, and balanced; putting others' needs and wants at a top-level of priority; listening; caring; and never hesitating to take action.

People pleaser: Someone who leans too much into the "I don't want to let you down" side of motivation and as a result ends up trying to please too many people. People pleasers operate with the best intentions, but they overextend themselves and can burn out easily because they often fail at trying to do too many things. Being a people pleaser isn't inherently a bad thing, but it's impossible to maintain over the long haul because you can't control how someone will react to you. You're best served trying to positively influence each person, without worrying about controlling an outcome.

Indifferent achiever: The indifferent achiever became a people leader purely because it was the next step after being promoted. Motivated by the hygiene factors of title, pay, and benefits, this is someone who doesn't really want to be a people manager but sees it as part of the responsibility that comes with moving up in an organization.

"Indifferent Achievers"

Over 20 years in business has shown me the "indifferent achiever" is much more common than people realize. It's part of the reason why some organizations struggle with leadership. People see becoming a people manager as the only path forward. They might actually rank it as one of their lower priorities, but it's part of the scope of the role they inherit when they're promoted. It's why I encourage business leaders to reconsider paths for individual contributors who want to stay as subject matter experts. Not everyone wants to be a leader, and leadership isn't for everyone. That's OK.

Earlier in my career, I had an indifferent achiever for a manager. He was a successful senior leader responsible for bringing in new deals to the business. Our relationship existed only on paper. We rarely met. I had to initiate meetings around my own development, with the exception of annual reviews. He couldn't contribute much meaningful feedback since there was little-to-no investment in how I was doing. All I could think was, "Who would ever want to be a part of a professional relationship this transactional in nature?"

Leaders who accept roles that have people management responsibilities but shirk them entirely are causing major issues for their organization. Think about it—engagement and retention are at the forefront of every HR conversation and on the minds of CEOs in every organization. Indifference is the opposite of engagement. It's why real conversations on commitment need to take place on a regular basis between an organization's leadership and its managers. Model what you want to see. Don't just warn about indifference; frequently engage and communicate how destructive this is to the long-term health of your organization.

Results-only: Results-only leaders are focused entirely on the bottom line. It's not about their employees' development. Rarely will they make time to discuss anything other than project tasks or deliverables and all one-on-ones are entirely tasks- and results-focused. To ignore the importance of business success would be foolish, but so is ignoring the duties of being a people leader.

Negative messenger: This is someone who only seems to deliver negative feedback or criticism. The only time you hear from them is when something has gone wrong. Their unwillingness to engage you in positive conversation shows they're not invested in you.

Decision-Making

A common thread I've observed in working with high achievers is how much accountability they take on to ensure they're doing the job well. They set huge goals and live with the pressures that come with trying to achieve them. They often achieve their goals, which demands focus and action. It requires everyday decision-making to keep moving forward. Indecision is crippling. When you're indecisive, you blame others. You come up with excuses. You don't hold yourself accountable. When you don't act—when you stay right where you are—you lose because you're not growing, and you're not learning.

Emotionally intelligent leaders are able to understand and process their emotions before making a decision. This helps them weigh all of the factors that could influence a positive or negative outcome. We face big decisions every day, and big decisions require that we have the confidence to act.

We can choose indecision—which leaves us right where we are—though this has a habit of affecting us in the long term. We can jump in hastily and make a decision without gathering all the facts. We may rely purely on our intuition without thinking ahead to the future. There are ramifications and ripple effects that both indecision and ineffective decision-making can have on our lives and our employees. It's critical to understand why you're making the decision you are and to lean on your core values to guide you. Decision-making takes into account variables such as:

- Relevant data and facts;
- Who is affected by your decision and how it will affect them;
- Understanding all of your options; and
- Counsel of others.

Now, let's take a closer look at how to prepare for making a decision.

Clear Your Mind

The best way to prepare for a big decision is to concentrate on clearing your mind. A great way to do this is to find time in solitude, where you can focus in the present moment without distractions.

A clear mind enables us to remove biases and manage worries, fears, and overly analytical thoughts. Here, we can slow the game down and get to the facts and information at hand. Sometimes, a new setting is helpful for changing your perspective and allowing you to refresh and revitalize your thoughts. It can help you to focus more effectively and consider emotional outcomes.

James D. Hess and Arnold C. Bacigalupo write: "The ability to assess the potential emotional outcomes and reactions of decisions can empower decision makers to predict the sentiment of those affected by decisions, thereby increasing the probability of a more positive decision outcome."[14]

We want to get to a place where we're better able to understand how emotions influence our decisions and to separate emotions from the facts. This enables us to objectively weigh all of the factors that will influence or affect our decisions. We take the aggregate of all the input we've received and rely on our intuition to help guide us toward doing what we feel is best.

In his book *Strategic Intuition*, Columbia Business School professor William Duggan discusses the breakdown of intuition in three ways: ordinary, expert, and strategic:

> Ordinary intuition is just a feeling, a gut instinct. Expert intuition is snap judgments, when you instantly recognize something familiar, the way a tennis pro knows where the ball will go from the arc and speed of the opponent's racket. . . .The third kind, strategic intuition, is not a vague feeling, like ordinary intuition. Strategic intuition is a clear thought. . . . That flash of insight you had last night might solve a problem that's been on your mind for a month.[15]

Ordinary intuition sometimes is the way to go. But when we have time to make a decision, strategic intuition is best. This helps us to think clearly and with mindfulness about what is in front of us. It enables us to extract that which matters most—the substance of what we feel is in our best interest—and guides us toward self-satisfaction.

Otherwise, we're just going on a whim.

Emotionally intelligent leaders know that decisions are influenced by both emotions and facts. Be willing to take a step back, reflect, and clear your mind. Separate emotions from the facts and understand how both guide and affect how you think and process each decision.

Value Each Person's Input

Always remember to involve a diverse, inclusive group of people in your team's decision-making process. Don't be too proud—seniority level or title shouldn't determine who has the best access to making a decision. The people on the frontline will often have the best information and will be in a position to give you the best answers. You need specifics. The level of granularity gained by the team members doing the work will be of most value in many instances.

Champion leaders make decisions that:

- Identify both the big picture and tactical needs;
- Are well-thought-out but not overly procrastinated on;
- Are well analyzed, anticipated, and identify the impacts; and
- Are then clearly communicated to the right people in a timely manner.

One technique I've used with groups is to ask each person to come up with their own independent assessment of what they feel is right, and to evaluate risks and impact. When everyone comes together, each person's hand can be shown. You avoid confirmation bias, preserve originality, and allow for each person's perspective during nonemergency instances.

Now that you've connected the CORD, you'll learn in Chapter 9 how to take greater ownership over building a high-performing team.

Connecting the CORD Exercise

Create your own CORD development plan for the next six months. List the

- Three ways you want to improve how you communicate;
- Three opportunities to convert into goals for your team;
- Three relationships you want to build; and
- Three techniques you can employ to become a better decision maker.

Use a quadrant to categorize these and track them each month to see how you're doing.

Champion's Checklist (Tools and Takeaways)

☑ Champion your team members' results and accomplishments.

☑ Widen the audience of who you connect with—find a way to have touchpoints with people all throughout your organization.

☑ Adopt a learner's mindset, and see each situation as an opportunity to learn something new.

☑ Make sure you over-communicate rather than under-communicate. Your team needs to clearly understand what you're saying.

☑ Involve a diverse group of people in the decision-making process.

Chapter 9

Adaptability and Responsibility (*Lead through Change and Take Ownership*)

"Change is the law of life. And those who look only to the past or present are certain to miss the future."

—President John F. Kennedy

Lisa Su's journey at Advanced Micro Devices (AMD) illustrates how technology, accountability, and adaptable leadership have come together to produce scintillating results. When she took over AMD in late 2014, the semiconductor company was foundering. After some huge staff layoffs, many wondered whether the long-established company would even survive. It would take a major leadership reclamation project to get AMD back on track. Fortunately, they turned to the right person.

Su implemented a vision that inspired innovation and accountability, while instilling consistency in the culture. She asked a tremendous amount of the engineers at AMD and set the bar high. She wanted them to design the fastest chips in the world. She got what she wanted. AMD continued to surge in value as more organizations started using AMD chips.

As we've learned so far, it's one thing to have a vision—it's another to unite an organization and adapt how you lead to a wide range of stakeholders. For a publicly traded company, it's an even greater challenge.

Recounting momentous decisions during her early days as CEO, Su said, "The most important thing for us back in 2014 was, first, choosing the right markets that were good for technology. It's not what you do today, but it's really what you do year after year, after year that people pay attention to."[1]

AMD made a "a big bet on high performance computing architecture, including powerful computer processors and graphics chips for gaming, artificial intelligence, supercomputing and other 'bleeding edge' technologies."[2]

Between 2017 and 2021, AMD's revenue more than tripled, growing from $5.3 billion to $16 billion. Su set a very high standard of expectations for results. She also became an extraordinarily effective communicator. She amplified the frequency and quality of her messaging, while communicating her vision to make sure everyone was on the same page. But it was a pivotal conversation with a senior leader that helped her adapt her communication style and build deeper connection with her employees.

Su said: "I was treating people the way I expected to be treated, and I don't expect anybody to ask me how I feel. I just expect to talk about the work. So he said, 'Lisa, you have to know that to get the best out of your people, different people need to be managed differently.'"

> That was a revelation to me. I say this now to my team: "Our jobs as leaders are to get 120 percent out of our teams. We're supposed to make the team better than they thought they could possibly be." The way to do that is to treat everyone as an individual, in terms of what they need to be successful and how they need to be coached.[3]

She's instilled the mindset in AMD employees that there's always that extra 5% everyone can do better. As AMD has grown over the past decade, they've hired more people who are motivated by that *better* mindset and mentality. This is a feeling and onus of responsibility that when catalyzed the right way, can produce tremendous results.

One way she encourages everyone to be better is by having an examination, or postmortem, of mistakes made, challenges encountered, and lessons learned. Su sees it as the leader's job to bring people together by providing guidance, while also motivating employees to recognize these improvements for themselves.

She said she looks for hunger and passion in employees and explained, "I want to understand the challenges they've taken on, and the risks they've taken in their career. . . . Look for those hardest problems and volunteer to help solve them."[4]

As you continue to lead through change, remember that exceptional results are possible when you communicate effectively and adapt how you communicate to each team member.

How to Create Accountability

Accountability is one of those words that can sometimes sound like nails screeching across an old-fashioned chalk board. It tends to make people feel uncomfortable and, at worst, is associated with negative consequences. The truth is, accountability isn't bad at all—it's essential to creating a high-performing team. It's the structural reinforcement that helps teams function at a high level. Let's focus on five steps for creating team accountability.

1. First, define exactly *what* each team member is responsible for.

   Defining roles and responsibilities helps each person understand how to truly own and outperform in their roles. It also creates transparency and collaboration that help each person learn how they can support each other.

When a team knows their roles and responsibilities and understands why they're doing what they're doing (purpose), you've established clear direction. This paves the road for people—who otherwise may not have communicated—to have natural, free-flowing conversations. The benefits here are endless around team building and innovation.

The goal is to always connect back to the vision and mission that you're looking to achieve. Aim to connect the tactical details to the strategic big picture. This will help to motivate your team members and keep them focused on what they're working to achieve.

A manufacturing organization that hired me to lead a series of team-building workshops for one of their business units was dealing with high turnover, dissension among employees, and lots of silos. Several employees told me they didn't understand how their work connected back to the organization's strategy. The piece that started to change everything was helping employees see the big picture and their role in it. Once this happened, more employees started actively engaging with one another.

It's impossible to sustain an accountable, empowered team in the long run if you don't clearly explain the inputs, outputs, and value of what your employees are producing. You need to give them the gift of strategic perspective and allow them to see it. Remember—seeing is believing when it comes to understanding roles and responsibilities in an organization.

2. Clearly communicate goals (SMART, or specific, measurable, achievable, relevant, and time-bound) *and* desired results. Be concise and clear. This is what backs up your expectations.

Repeat and consistently message these goals and results—keep this top priority.

3. Be candid and clear in your guidance and how you share information. For example, some people may be better equipped to handle certain clients or roles; ask everyone to take responsibility and make the commitment to their piece. This helps position and put each person in the best fit for delivering for each client.
4. Provide feedback and maintain consistency for how you communicate throughout each process. If steps in a process are not being executed properly, work with your leaders and team leads to ensure this gets fixed. Pinpoint the key areas of quality (communication, planning, execution, and monitoring work), and stay on top of these. A feedback culture is a winning culture. (You can refer to Chapter 2 for guidance on how to deliver stellar feedback.)
5. Positively recognize successes and celebrate the wins. When someone succeeds, provide them with more opportunities (responsibilities, not just tasks). Ask them what new opportunities they want. They've earned them.

Putting a timestamp on certain needs is critical. This is not micromanaging. This is holding people accountable. You can do it with kindness, purpose, and respect.

People need clearer direction at times. There's nothing wrong with providing someone with steps for how to do something. In the name of Situational Leadership, you can calibrate that per person. This is earned by the relationship-building time you spend connecting with each person. Be informed and understand just how much you need to communicate—and how much you don't.

Adapting to a Changing Business Landscape

Think about how much has changed in only four years' time in business and in life. During any prolonged period of change, it's critical to keep an open mind and to be adaptable. Optimize your focus on driving your business forward and instilling confidence in your team.

This is the most important time in business history to communicate effectively, frequently, and with heart to make sure your people know precisely where you're leading them. It's also a call for you to strategize on how to adapt your communications to the needs of multiple generations of the workforce. Individualizing your messaging to a younger generation of employees may mean using more digital tools. When connecting with baby boomers or Gen X, you may be best suited to have face-to-face or verbal communications. Understand differences, build trust by showing you care, and foster a culture of respect for one another.

Countless companies have faced adversity. Every life-changing moment and adversity is an opportunity for us to be proactive—not reactive. This doesn't mean changing your entire strategy, but it could mean making some modifications. Maybe it's about modifying the way you connect with your customers.

More customers are reticent to spend on nonessential purchases. Business leaders need to understand this and adapt. Offering incentives is always a way to go, but this is also a wise time to personalize outreach and communications to your existing clients. It's an opportunity to look at what you do well and figure out how that translates to new market needs. Following the global shutdown related to the coronavirus in March 2020, we saw companies such as Fanatics go from making baseball uniforms to making masks and other medical gear for nurses and hospital workers.[5] Car manufacturers such as Tesla altered their assembly lines to go from making automobiles to making ventilators.[6]

During periods of change, the impulse for so many is fear. Some organizations are afraid to change because they haven't acknowledged the change in the first place. This is rooted in fear and to some degree a lack of preparedness. Change requires courage, gumption, and massive effort to maneuver out of the old and into the new way of doing business. It's not easy, but when you see change as part of the rhythm of business and accept it for what it is, it becomes easier to process. The choice to change is always one that we have in our control.

As the business landscape and how we communicate changes, we must be willing to adapt. This is the essence of emotional intelligence and what leadership is all about. As a leader, adaptability isn't optional. There's no avoiding adversity. Emotionally intelligent leaders know how to adapt to adversity in the form of crises, attrition, economic downturns, and decreases in morale.

Mary Barra, whose story we learned about in Chapter 4, talked about the power of adapting and how it begins with the way we behave: "We can all change our behavior. Every day, I can work to demonstrate the behaviors the senior leaders, the top 300 leaders in the company [are doing]."[7]

Staying positive and modeling the behavior you want to see in others is essential. Accepting the circumstances for what they are and turning to problem solving and process improvement allow you to make things better. For example, if you have two team members or cross-functional partners who aren't getting along, or aren't even speaking to each other, step in, call out the problem, and collaborate to resolve the conflict. In a situation like this, coordinate first with the leader of the other team. Get on the same page. Mediate a three-way discussion and be inquisitive, open-minded, and empathetic.

Great leaders ask themselves the question, "How are we getting better today?" Then, they get to work and keep moving forward. Staying stuck is the enemy of progress.

Questions for reflection:

- What are ways that you've proactively adapted to change as a leader?
- What does leadership responsibility mean to you?
- What's one "common sense" piece of guidance you can provide to a team member? To yourself?
- What have you learned from exit interviews (when employees have left your organization) that can help you adapt to drive better employee engagement?

Meeting People Where They Are

The more clearly people understand the organizational structure and communication structure for accountability, the more efficient they will be. You need to have a consistent process for what you do so your team can execute successfully. You can continue to solidify this for your team. Here are some examples:

- Everyone shows up on time for meetings with laptops closed and phones down.
- If you need an answer or input of information, be persistent and follow up.
- Keep the people who need to be informed in the loop.

What matters is the personal level of responsibility you and your team have to your clients and one another. Accountability begins with holding yourself accountable to a high standard of results and client service. You bring that to your clients and build a relationship that is tailored to what they need. Bring that same accountability to your company and your colleagues. We all have a responsibility to ourselves, to our clients, and to each other. Always think, "How can I deliver exactly what they need and want, and adapt when needed to make sure I'm staying on top of things?" Keeping this top of mind is what will lead us to success and huge growth.

Finding the time for ideas and inspiration is what leads to personal accountability that influences the way you lead. I talk a lot with clients about having "methods of magnitude," which are really the code you live by and professional standards you uphold. I set these up for my own business, for things such as client coaching calls, business meetings, speaking preparation, and even writing this book. In the same way values form our bedrock foundation, these methods of magnitude are cornerstone pillars that guide our actions.

You could try this with your team or colleagues. Let's use individual relationships as an example. You can modify this to make it work for you:

- Connect for 30 minutes once per week.
- Dedicate five minutes in every meeting to allow for questions and coaching.
- Always have at least one touchpoint per day, even if it's a quick text or instant message to say hi.
- Send valuable "How-to tools," videos, curated articles, thoughts/ideas, and motivational/inspirational messages.

By doing this, you create an objective standard you can aspire to attain each day. You model the leadership you want to influence others to learn from and use in their interactions with others.

If You See Something, Say Something

Several years ago when I lived in New York City, there were yellow signs that were ubiquitous on the subway, at subway stations, and on street signposts. They said, "If you see something, say something." It was a call to speak up and report dangerous activity if you happened to witness it. The same saying can be applied in leadership.

Champion leaders are masters of the obvious, which isn't a smart-aleck way of doing things. It's really a commonsense approach to helping others. One of the smartest things that a manager can do is compassionately and kindly point out things that their employees need to fix. It may be things that you see, but are blind spots for your team members. The fact is, all of us can struggle on occasion with self-awareness.

During a stressful or busy period, we may not see something that could seem obvious to someone else. If we could only receive the input that would help us change, we'd be much better off. This could be things such as not speaking up enough in meetings or speaking too quickly. It could also be that someone is too verbose or commanding in how they deliver direction or maybe that someone isn't building relationships, but instead burning bridges. Wouldn't you want someone to point this out if you were guilty of it, but didn't realize you were doing it?

Like with well-timed praise, be selective in when you do this for others. Get a sense for how someone is doing emotionally and ask them first, "Would it be OK with you if I gave you some feedback that could help you?" Be willing to point out the obvious things. Give commonsense guidance.

If You Don't Know Something, Say You Don't Know and Find the Solution

Author and entrepreneur Gary Vaynerchuk said, "When you're humble enough not to put yourself on a pedestal, you follow your curiosities, you're accountable to your mistakes, and you remember that no matter how much you've accomplished, you're still 'just getting started.'"[8]

In that spirit of humility meeting accountability, recognize there is power in not knowing something. This is when curiosity takes over and our desire to get answers, and help others, kicks in. We all take a lot of pride in knowing things, but what happens when we're asked a question and we don't know the answer? This shouldn't feel like a crushing blow. Instead, see it as an opportunity. Own the "not knowing," find out the answer, and come back to deliver it.

When we let pride take over, we tend to be long-winded and we talk much longer than we need to, without offering a solution. I coach leaders on always shooting straight; it's amazing how confident and assertive we can be by admitting that we don't know something. You won't always have the answers, but you have the ability to find them out.

Finding Calm and Poise to Guide You

Finding time for a daily inspirational routine to rally you and give you the energy you need for each day helps immensely during periods of change when you need to adapt. This is about achieving what famous psychologist Abraham Maslow highlighted in his *hierarchy of needs*—self-actualization. I encourage clients to find time, ideally in the first part of their day, to brainstorm and imagine positive, inspiring thoughts that evoke emotions such as success, happiness, exhilaration, love, peace of mind, and true satisfaction. One way to look at it is this—think about what you're truly working for. What are the end results—what are the greatest rewards that you want from your hard work?

Find time for solitude where you can process your thoughts and strike up creative ideas. The leader of an organization I once worked for frequently said, "Think *big* thoughts." Focus on positive, stimulating thoughts such as achieving a big goal, making a difference in someone's life, and helping someone to get a leg up on their upward career ascension. The energy created from positive thinking in solitude is immense.

Mike Erwin writes in *Harvard Business Review*, "Having the discipline to step back from the noise of the world is essential to staying focused . . . solitude [is] a state of mind, a space in which to focus one's own thoughts without distraction—and where the mind can work through a problem on its own."[9]

We all have reminders these days—on our smartphones, our cars, and yes, even the old-school method of the refrigerator note or Post-it on our desks. Remind yourself of what you've accomplished and who you are. Use reminders to see all of the wonderful blessings you already have in your life—and the positive contributions and accomplishments you've achieved. A big part of having an inspirational routine is embracing the process of realizing all that's going well.

Fostering Trust and Reducing Feeling Overwhelmed

Providing leadership accountability and instilling a culture of ownership needs to be balanced with a careful awareness of recognizing when your team members feel overwhelmed. When team members put too much self-imposed pressure on themselves, it can lead to feeling overwhelmed, which leads to stress. We cannot think as clearly and function as well when our brains are overloaded with too much information and unrealistic expectations. Remember to build yourself up over time and be conscious of building your team members up for the responsibilities that they tackle. Encourage them to speak up if they feel overwhelmed. Promote taking breaks and finding restorative time to reenergize and recharge.

It's a reminder that we need to meet people where they're at emotionally and mentally and to form our connection around responsibility there. Nurture relationships by bringing people along and modeling championship leadership for them.

Setting Modes of Communication

As we covered in Chapter 6, the need for in-person connection is real—not just for innovation and results but for building relationships. There are powerful social and emotional wellness benefits that come from connecting with others. But the hybrid model of work for many organizations is a long-term reality. For some full-time remote employees, the need to stay connected and find virtual collaboration opportunities is critical for individual and team success. How organizations adapt to the hybrid and virtual workplace will define their success going forward. Some guidance herein:

- Ensure your team's technology needs are satisfied. Everything hinges on the ability to have a working Internet connection and a functioning computer, tablet, monitor, and phone.
- Don't just jump right into status updates and progress reports on the team's work during meetings. Ask them how they're doing! Make an honest effort once per day to check in with each member of your team by video, phone, email, or instant message. Be sincere and understand that giving autonomy is a balancing act. Don't micromanage, but don't be too distant. Recognize opportunities to show appreciation, share news, and see how you can be of help.
- Know your tools and set some ground rules. Leverage tools such as Microsoft Teams, Slack, and Basecamp. Most importantly, set very clear expectations around deliverables, check-ins, and weekly performance goals. This will take thought and effort, as well as a re-commitment to your company values.
- Build a network of trust. You won't always know for certain that someone is working when they say they are. Start with trust first. If you feel they're missing the mark on deadlines or giving you reasons to doubt, then follow up.

- Focus on the productivity criteria. Schedule check-ins, but understand each team member won't be able to connect every minute of the day.

By pulling back on some things, you'll earn the trust of your team. Remember to adapt and be flexible as things continue to change.

14 Reasons Why Your Best Employees Are Leaving

Every organization needs to deal with succession planning that prepares it for when employees leave for new opportunities elsewhere. We've all noticed more attrition over the past several years as the modern workplace has changed. Work flexibility is here to stay, and a hybrid balance can be a good thing for many organizations. But there are other reasons why employees leave. Knowing what these reasons are will help you adapt and identify successors for key roles. It will also help you to identify high-potential employees. Here are 14 reasons why your best employees are leaving.

1. Pay (of course!);
2. Work flexibility;
3. Lack of vision and engagement from the organization's leadership;
4. Their leader/manager doesn't take the time to get to know them on a personal level;
5. Little to no managerial interest in their professional advancement; they don't have a coach/mentoring relationship at the organization;
6. Lack of upward mobility, which is often caused by:

a. An overemphasis on hiring externally to replace or create new roles and not rewarding high performers; and

b. An outdated or incongruent promotion progression is in place; some advance in different ways than others, creating dissension.

7. Respect and recognition:

a. While rewards programs matter, they're a small piece of the pie. The greatest value for many employees isn't receiving a $50 gift card to Target. It's in receiving an award. It's being mentioned in the company newsletter or having a senior level executive recognize them in front of their coworkers. It's in listening and allowing that person's voice to be heard.

b. Without this, employees are left to wonder: Is my leadership paying attention?

8. They don't understand their importance to the organization (big picture).

9. Their ideas aren't heard. They're not empowered enough to feel their ideas matter.

10. Same old, same old (promises that things will change—and then they don't).

11. Oligarchy syndrome: Power by a few makes employees feel that they can't break through.

12. Work-life balance. They are overworked, and the organization doesn't realize it.

13. No time for creativity/professional development outside of daily job responsibilities. In other words, there is a lack of innovation or lack of acceptance of innovation and ideas—particularly on the frontline of the organization. Many employees want to do

meaningful things to improve the organization's culture or operating procedures—outside of their core responsibilities.

14. They don't have enough positive relationships (negative culture).

The biggest thing you have in your control as a leader is being the best that you can be for your team. Overwhelmingly, employees are looking for leaders who care about them. They want a feeling of belonging. The most direct point of contact that any employee has in a company is the person who sits right next to them and of course, their manager. I think of Herzberg's two-factor theory. While money and job security absolutely matter, it's the motivators such as respect and recognition that make a huge difference in why employees stay with an organization. When a leader pays attention to his or her employees, those employees notice! Results follow.

How You Can Adapt Early to Meet Employees' Needs

Caring leaders take the time to get to know their employees first (if possible) during the interview process and then immediately after. This is an enduring relationship. Caring leaders invest their time in getting to know the strengths and areas their employees are looking to improve, as well as what their personal and professional interests are. They understand what their employees' short- and long-term plans are—in fact, they partner with them to develop them.

Champion leaders are coaches. They focus on values, connecting them with learning resources, as well as people at the company that can help their development. They do this from the get-go because they know it's at the heart of crafting an incredible employee experience that leads to a culture of connection.

It doesn't take long for a motivated, high-performing employee to understand what is and *isn't* possible for advancement at their company. What's remarkable is how few companies and organizations clearly define this path forward. If there's no performance management process in place—no clearly defined and presented process for promotion—then upbeat employees will lose interest and start looking elsewhere.

Build in career development conversations early on in someone's tenure. Be open-minded in creating a work flexibility policy that rewards performance. Do the best that you can to show someone what their path forward looks like at the company. There are no guarantees and no playbook that details precisely how to get promoted—we know this. What you can do is help your employees focus on high-value goals that increase the probability that they will reach that next level. Articulate this vision and help them to see themselves in it. Tie it to the big picture goals for your team and the entire organization. You have a lot of control and influence over the employee experience.

Take a look again at this list of why employees are leaving. Ask yourself, "What can I control, and what can I influence?" Then, take actions that consistently make your workplace an engaging and inspiring place to be.

Creating Ownership

When I think about creating ownership as a leader, I think about one word: responsibility. This means that you take charge of making success happen and you adapt to any changes that need to be made. You have to demand the best from yourself to build your responsibility strength. Competitive greatness is about challenging yourself (and challenging your team members) to be your best. High achievers want to be challenged. When you do this with compassion, you build confidence in your team members. You become more confident in your leadership capabilities. You see each new gain as powering you forward toward your next step of growth. Be open to how others can help you and be humble to allow them to help you.

Being responsible is about embracing a game plan that starts with a foundation of personal accountability, like we saw in Chapter 2. Jocko Willink talks about responsibility in his book *Extreme Ownership*: "On any team, in any organization, all responsibility for success and failure rests with the leader. The leader must own everything in his or her world. There is no one else to blame. The leader must acknowledge mistakes and admit failures, take ownership of them, and develop a plan to win."[10]

I'd add that it's important to strike a balance between what you take home, so to speak, and what you leave behind each day. It's never a good thing to put too much blame on yourself. It affects your mindset and can destroy self-confidence. Whether you've made a mistake or absorbed a team failure, take your time to process it, regroup, and move forward to the next opportunity with confidence.

Also remember to take ownership over your successes. Finding this equanimity of self-confidence helps you to not get too high—or too low. I've coached some leaders who process their thoughts and say, *"I'm an accomplished leader who's well respected, but I struggle with success. I sometimes don't see myself as successful, even when others do. It comes and goes, and sometimes I struggle with seeing myself the way others see me."*

We're all going to face the "Sunday Scaries" from time to time, and yes, sometimes it feels easier to not want to own the responsibilities that come with leading a team. It's OK to doubt yourself from time to time—this leads to introspection and moves you toward the foundational pillars of purpose and values. This strengthens your desire to take responsibility. The most important topic that many leadership conversations boil down to is confidence. Even the leaders at the top of their professions struggle with self-confidence at times. It's a reminder that taking ownership and building strong, resolute inner-belief each day helps us to boost confidence.

Smooth Transitions

Adaptability and the will to change begins in our minds with how we process our thoughts. Our thoughts and emotions are always evolving. Understand and recognize that emotions (negative and positive) will come and go. They're impermanent. When you become more adaptable and agile in your mind, you'll be able to transition smoothly to what's next. Adaptable leaders are able to context-switch efficiently by compartmentalizing their emotions. They move forward from one thing to the next by accepting both positive and negative emotions and managing them effectively.

Adaptability is a skill set that you can work on and teach to others. You can do this for yourself with the knowledge from this chapter, and you can help your employees recognize the importance of adapting and taking ownership of their responsibilities. Provide them with the vision of how this connects back to the big picture. Inspire them to grow, learn, and improve every day.

Adaptability and Responsibility Exercise

One for you:

Create two columns, one for what you can control and another for what you can influence as a leader. Within the columns, you're welcome to create categories (e.g., projects, people, processes), if that helps. Create a list for each with a plan for how you will take action. What's in your control are outcomes you have total ability to directly affect. What you can influence are outcomes or behaviors; it's how you go about inspiring, persuading, and motivating without direct control. Gaining an understanding of the two will help you become more adaptable for how you lead.

One for your team:

Leaning on the "own" portion of Own, Partner, Delegate (from Chapter 5), create a competitive challenge for your team members. Ask them to define success for three tasks they currently own and to list examples of stretch opportunities they'd like to own. Encourage them to list the key ingredients for success in how they'd accomplish each task.

Champion's Checklist (Tools and Takeaways)

- ☑ The most powerful leadership is leadership by example.
- ☑ Understand what you control and what you can influence. Own each with maximum responsibility.
- ☑ Build-in time in one-on-one conversations to ask employees what you can do to meet their needs.
- ☑ Be daring and speak up when you can help someone. Be courageous, and acknowledge when you don't yet know something. Then, figure out a solution.
- ☑ Evaluate your strategic direction from time to time, and recognize what you may need to do to change.

Chapter 10

The Voice of the Champion Leader (*The Little Things That Make a Big Difference*)

One vitally important lesson that I've learned in my two-decade professional career: it's wise to listen to successful people who have thrived in their roles and lifted others up. So, in that spirit, that is exactly how this chapter is set up. I've interviewed thousands of world-class leaders over the years, some of whom are featured throughout the chapters. The interviews in this chapter are specific, deep-cuts with leadership guidance from senior leaders in a variety of industries. These insights are intended to help you increase your emotional intelligence, navigate through change and build high-performing teams.

There are also select stories, lessons, and "little things" that I've found make a big difference in leading and living the life we want to live. Take them in and see what you can learn and use for yourself.

And Now for a Few Words . . .

Stacie Bloom

Chief Research Officer, New York University

Stacie Bloom sees a direct linkage between champion leaders and a desire for continuous learning, growth, and development.

She believes people committed to leadership who, "rise up the ranks in the profession are the ones that really focus on the nuances of emotional intelligence."[1]

She discussed the importance of lifelong learning.

> You learn from faux pas, mistakes, teaching yourself to be prepared, and knowing what questions to ask people.
>
> I like to think, "How are my social skills going to be better at this board of directors retreat than the last one?" It's about getting better.

> We know we can learn throughout our lives—our brain is adapting all of the time.
>
> We're lifelong learners. Leading with emotional intelligence and becoming more self-confident means making a concerted effort to be self-aware, to self-regulate and to always want to improve who you are.

She talked about the core value of authenticity.

> I think about how much energy must go into being *inauthentic*. In other words, presenting a front of who you are not. As a result, it requires a lot of mental energy. I want to spend my mental energy on the things that truly matter. We're not limitless in what we can do neurologically. If you're spending time trying to be someone you're not, you lose the space to learn. You don't have as much time to have self-control, resilience, perseverance.
>
> I'm where I am today because people have invested in me.

She said she created a leadership model that is very people-centric.

> I believe people are at the center of everything in leadership —I care deeply about authentic relationships.

It's relationships that have enabled her to rise and become a highly respected senior leader at NYU. Formal leadership training has really helped her. She took Doug Conant's HALI: Higher Ambition Leadership Institute program. She said she learned a lot about empathy and people-based leadership.

> My higher ambition is to support other women and underrepresented people in science, and help them foster careers where they can be very successful. Science has been an historically dominated male field and a very difficult environment for women and people of color to be successful and break into. I want to change that.

She thinks about paying things forward and being in a position she loves, and sees it as an onus to "pay this back a million times forward and to do this for other people."

Chiho Kelly

Assurance Managing Director, Ernst & Young (EY) LLP

Chiho Kelly has found that showing appreciation and recognition, along with clear direction, makes a huge difference in how we connect with our teams.

> I've learned the nuances of communicating artfully—telling my teams what to do with clear direction. Sharing positive compliments, empowering their belief that they can do it.
>
> Be quick to tell people that they've done a great job—take the time to recognize their efforts and accomplishments. Inspire people to go above and beyond what they think they can do.
>
> Lean into positivity and say things like, "You can try this next time," as opposed to telling someone they didn't do well or wrong. This makes a huge difference.[2]

She's also a leader by example who's willing to be there side-by-side with her team if they need her help. Showing your team that you're willing to do what you're asking them to do is another hallmark of a champion leader.

> If there's an urgent or last-minute matter, I roll my sleeves up and help them out. I'm not afraid to jump into the details and support my people when I need to. If I tell them to do something, I'm not just being their boss, I will help out and be there with them when I need to.
>
> Be available, be flexible. Remember to find time to take care of yourself and prioritize what's most important in your personal and professional life.

Michael G. Johnson

President and CEO, Harlem Educational Activities Fund (HEAF)

Michael G. Johnson's career has spanned working in the private, public, and nonprofit sectors. His wisdom herein is both for executives leading with emotional intelligence, and guidance for early-career employees on the importance of preparing, learning, and putting your skill set together.

He talked about the importance of building relationships.[3]

> I have to individually relate to a variety of personalities; I have to deeply understand what the CFO or the development officer is feeling (understanding their role, what they're going through). Knowing how to put people in the right place to be able to succeed and giving them the space they need to execute is vital.
>
> During a crisis, you have to show and demonstrate compassion, the ability to move forward, to motivate and encourage.

This is ultimately where leaders shine—in these moments of adversity and challenge.

Whether in good or bad times, it's so important to consistently acknowledge, praise and recognize the people you lead.

When I join the calls and meetings throughout the organization and communicate with people, I see myself as the Chief Motivator.

On growing, adapting, and being ready for opportunities:

One thing I've learned is the ability to adapt and move forward—to not let something fester. Once it's over, it's over. Recognize it's time to move on. Don't let something become baggage.

I'd encourage younger leaders not to be driven by a title. Ask yourself, "Am I ready on the emotional intelligence side of things?" There were times in my career where I knew I had the ability and IQ, but knew I needed to grow my EQ. Have a barometer and check on the EQ side. You can't just be good at your job—you have to know how to communicate and help others.

Before you even step into a leadership role, identify your "support system" that will help position you for success. This could be a mentor or a coach. Find someone you can learn from, who will push you. Mentors have made a huge difference in my career.

He shared his thoughts on "little things" that matter and he discussed how important it is to understand the history of an organization.

Be sensitive, compassionate and understanding of where people and the organization have come from. Ask yourself, "Am I ready to manage and handle the complexities that come with it?" When you first come into an organization, be prepared to meet people, learn the history and gain an understanding and respect of where people are coming from that helps you to lead better.

Throughout my career, I've always found the time to get involved in the "little things" because I know how much those details matter.

Senior Financial Services Leader

Senior Vice President and Market Leader, global financial services firm

He started by telling me: "The most successful entrepreneurs and business leaders have an advanced understanding of people." It's that spirit that has guided how he leads.

On leadership:

> How I was taught to treat others (managing up, managing down, my peers, mentoring) is what moved me to leadership. I always felt that the team vision was an important part of what was guiding me, even as an individual contributor. I credit that to playing sports and identifying with a team-first mindset.
>
> EQ has been a crucial part of what has guided my conversations and my decision making. I wanted to be seen as a resource—when you're a resource, people will see you as a leader.
>
> Let's get the group together, let's share ideas, there are benefits to working together.

What's shaped his mindset has been having a positive outlook. He believes it's helped attract others to want to connect with him. From a journey standpoint, his mindset is the key to how he treats others.

I believe in being positive as often as possible, without being Pollyannaish. That will help others see the good in your intentions. A lot of having a positive outlook is the environment that you create for yourself. My upbringing, my peer group, who I've surrounded myself with and building relationships have allowed me to have a sounding board. You get to choose who those people are. When you have that support group around you, it's a game changer.

One thing you cannot fake are your intentions. If my intentions are, "I enjoy helping people"—and I do—I feel that is what I'm doing each day.

There is a certain confidence that I've built in myself to feel there is an opportunity for me to help, add value, make the situation better—sometimes that's putting someone in a good mood, making them laugh, encouraging them, comforting them during a tough time. The opportunity is there to help others as a leader.

You need to have an internal belief system, which I believe is a part of my core values system. My instincts are, when I'm around a situation there might be an opportunity for me to help. I come from a family where my mom was a nurse and Dad a police officer, they were a big part of the community. I've always wanted to be someone to help solve problems and help others do that for themselves.

On looking out for others:

As technology evolves, an important part of what we do is using data to help us make informed decisions. That might be knowing the "little things" that will lift people up personally. Could be a birthday, work anniversary, etc. Our ability to process data is what helps me to focus on things like recognition and gratitude toward people to encourage continued success. And then, how can I coach others to get on track with that data. The data can help me to individualize the way I relate to people. That will never change.

Not just to send someone an email congratulating them on "40 years." Person #1 may want a one-on-one breakfast. Person #2 may want to celebrate with everyone. Your ability as a leader to understand those nuances is what builds the culture of your organization.

If it's in your organization's culture to recognize people in a certain way that is consistently personalized—that can trickle down from the top. You can always go deeper—even if you're running a larger organization. It's the same principle with clients. I think you can delegate, create, and build that culture that gives back to itself.

We all have a tendency to do things faster; it's super-important to slow down. Get to know your people. Understand what's important to them, and understand what's going on in their lives as best you can. When you can emotionally connect and make an impact with people, where you're dialing in on things that make people feel valued—things that are personalized—then you've truly gotten through to them.

Brad Gien

Director of Operations, Inotiv

Brad Gien has become an industry leader and highly respected subject and functional matter expert by communicating effectively and understanding how to inspire and help his team members.

He provided some thoughts on his early-career leadership development.[4]

One of the biggest things that I learned early in my career—by working in multiple roles in my industry—was what not to do first.

Some of my biggest fears when I first started out were, "Why are they not talking to me?" and "Should I ask for help?" I recognized how to understand and empathize with people and I gained the courage to ask for help.

I recognized that an organization cannot be successful unless it understands "Why" it's doing what it's doing.

On the importance of listening and individualizing the way he communicates:

One of the things that I see as a huge strength of leaders is listening more than talking. It's having empathy for the people you lead. I try and empower people to be great listeners.

Leading is not an exact science and you need to constantly evolve and adapt. For every person you lead, you need to approach them differently. Some people find that daunting, but it's the best way. You need to understand what's going on in someone's life and their career aspirations in order to build a relationship with them. This helps them to become more productive and better, future leaders.

There's a way to motivate and lead people to get the most out of them and to develop them to their full potential versus just managing them to do a job.

On change, risk and building an inclusive decision-making process:

My ability to adapt has earned me the respect of my peers, because I've been able to recognize change, modify a new plan and move forward.

I found myself gravitating toward people who weren't risk averse, but instead who were willing to try something new. What I've learned is people can be really afraid of change—and the risks associated with making changes. I understand it's a risk to change things that are proven already and have perhaps worked. But I love the curiosity and probing that comes with being willing to change and strive to do something better. Providing vision of the targeted results in advance always helps.

One thing I love to do is to involve people in the decision-making process. Getting them to buy-in and be involved in a decision inspires them to try harder to make things work. We usually get there because we're all-in.

Wisdom from the "Wizard of Westwood," Coach John Wooden

"I'm gonna show you how to put on your shoes and socks."[5]

Coach John Wooden was a man focused on the details. For an incredible stretch between 1963 and 1975, the UCLA men's basketball team captured the NCAA championship a stunning 10 times, including seven seasons in a row. Coach Wooden was fortunate to coach some extraordinary players such as Lew Alcindor (later known as Kareem Abdul-Jabbar), Bill Walton, Gail Goodrich, and Sidney Wicks. But having great players doesn't always guarantee superior results. Championships are won in the details—the fundamentals of the game that can be taught, emphasized, and lived by each day.

Wooden didn't want his players to develop blisters. Blisters meant you could miss time, which meant his best players could miss key minutes that added up to a game's victory. Those missed minutes came from socks being put on too loosely and sometimes from wearing basketball shoes that were just a half-size too big.

Wooden famously taught all of his players how to put their socks and shoes on at the beginning of every basketball season. He made sure the socks were neatly smoothed out, shoes appropriately laced, and everything fitted perfectly. This was at UCLA, a school that was winning the college basketball national championship nearly every season! Wooden understood that the fundamentals of the game were vital to success. Why not start at a very basic level?

But even more pertinent, he was trying to give his team every advantage that he could. He was attempting to reduce their mistakes—the silly, often overlooked turnovers that can detract from our overall performance.

More than that, of course, there was a coach getting his players to see there would be no shortcuts, no key details overlooked. To have a high-performing team, you can apply the same "little things" to how you lead. You don't need to overly obsess over things that aren't important. Instead, identify the scope of what does matter to the success of your team and how attention to detail makes the difference between success and failure.

Your character and your ability to apply yourself with consistency are inextricably linked. Champion leaders and performers are consistently great. This begins with a positive growth mindset and is backed up by a hard, intelligent work ethic. It's not a sometimes thing. It's an *all* the time thing. It happens in the workplace. It happens at home. It's when you're dealing with friends or in public at events. And perhaps most significantly, it's the way you behave and act when no one is watching.

That person you look at in the mirror—they're going to want to know whether you held yourself accountable to a higher standard of conduct and performance. When you can honestly say that you've done your best, that you've given your all, and that you've consciously made the effort to eliminate the negatives that hold you back, you'll know you're on the journey to greatness.

Just remember to put your socks and shoes on the right way. Every detail matters.

The Feeling You Get

There's a special feeling we get when we shop at local mom-and-pop stores, isn't there? It's a personalized experience—one that is crafted with love and care. I've always enjoyed doing business at local delis, coffee shops, auto repair shops, bakeries, and diners. There's one particular barbershop that holds a very special place in my heart.

In my hometown—Rockville Centre, New York—Mr. José Dominguez owns a local barbershop that he's operated for over 55 years. He emigrated from Cuba in 1968 and fled to find freedom for himself and his family, to become a business owner.

So why do I love walking into his shop? I love a nice, smooth haircut, don't get me wrong. But that's not the biggest reason. It's the way I feel when I walk in the door. The little bells that chime when the door opens. The train that rounds the train track that hangs from the ceiling. As I turn to the right, I see a shrine on the wall, next to the windows, that memorializes 50 people from my hometown who lost their lives during the September 11 terrorist attacks.

I see my picture and the pictures of childhood friends in dozens of frames that encircle the interior walls of the shop. It's the smiles and head nods I get from both the patrons and barbers. The huge handshake and hug from José. I feel home. It's one of the best feelings in the world. And let's be honest—it has nothing to do with getting a haircut.

But it has *everything* to do with getting a haircut in José's barbershop.

Those are the "little things" that make the difference between attracting customers and employees and retaining them. I still fly to New York to visit friends and family, and I always make a point to stop and visit José's barbershop. Those are the magnetic moments that stick with us. It's what connection is all about. The experience he's created is special. It's something to think about for your own organization and team. Think about ways you can craft a memorable experience where your employees—and customers—come together, enjoy it, and keep coming back for more.

Delivering What Your Team Needs

If you're struggling as a leader right now, here's a great way to take inventory through self-awareness: start focusing on the "little things" your organization and team need to be successful.

In other words—what does your team or organization *not* have right now that you have the skill set to provide? How can you deliver it? Sometimes, it's less about the core pieces such as making the extra sale or creating a dazzling presentation. It might mean listening to a team member and being there for them when they're down.

It might be developing a new marketing strategy that worked for you in the past and could work now. It might be harnessing the power of a new software tool that can improve the way your team communicates. Be innovative. Rely on your strengths. Think about your abilities, and ask yourself, "Does my team need this?"

Do the "little things." Do those little—yet very important—things that others aren't willing to do. Everyone will take notice. And you'll be a difference maker. What are those "little things" for you right now as a leader?

Champion leaders have an eye for these kinds of "little things":

- A desire to help others;
- Punctuality;
- Lightening the mood during a challenging time;
- Self-respect and respect toward others; and
- Knowing when it's time to get to work and when it's time to focus on socializing for the benefit of the group.

Ego Is a Tightrope Act

Ego is a tightrope act you will walk personally, professionally, publicly, and privately your whole life. Achieve success of any kind, and you'll find external recognition for your accomplishments. You'll feel good on the inside. Ideally, this will lead to confidence and perseverance, rather than an inflated sense of self-worth, which only leads to the pursuit of the next high.

This high can never truly be satisfied by any accomplishment. It's driven by pride and ego, which will push you further away from what you desire at your inner core. Ego is something we always need to stay on top of. The way we conquer the negative side of our ego is with emotional intelligence—keen self-awareness, empathy, and self-management. Emotional intelligence helps us to understand our ego and manage it accordingly.

Ego can lead to overconfidence. Being overly confident often leads to mistakes. Dr. Joyce Ehrlinger, formerly of Washington State University, in a combined study with professors from Stanford and Florida State University, found overconfidence can lead to poor decisions:

A little bit of overconfidence can be helpful, but larger amounts of overconfidence can lead people to make bad decisions and to miss out on opportunities to learn.[6]

Particularly with social media, we want to share our measures of success. All of us, even the most introverted among us, want to feel appreciated and recognized by our peers. For some, it's easy to manifest a cult of personality, where it seems our whole world revolves around how great we are. We get frustrated when others don't recognize how amazing we are!

With ego, when you keep it in check, you're doing the right thing. When you go too far, losing control, it's not what might hurt you on the outside but what might affect you on the inside that could disrupt your behavior. Damage to your reputation can certainly hurt. I tend to focus more on character. The worst damage is self-inflicted. It's dangerous when you corrupt your own sense of value and self-worth.

Keeping it real—we all have an ego that we need to keep in check. Be humble and use your energy to help others. This leads to a more fulfilling, optimistic, and happy way of life.

Strive to Be Pro

One of the best lessons I've learned in life is this: professionals find a way to put in their best effort. All the time.

Please, don't confuse this with best performance. Or masterpiece. Nope. I'm talking about what 50% of the battle truly is: showing up. Then, mustering up the energy, effort, heart, soul, attitude, and grit to get the job done. Whatever that job may be. So I ask you, wherever you are in your career right now: Are you showing up and doing your best every day? The reality is, you have complete control over this. But that doesn't make it easy.

Some of us end up in jobs we don't like. Some of us end up doing work we love, and yet still struggle to bring our best every day. Sure, there are a litany of reasons—maybe, depending on your point of view, excuses. Some are more valid than others.

- Too tired;
- Anxious;
- Competing priorities; and
- Don't have the time.

In the end, if you want to be the best professional and have a long-lasting career, you really need to bring it every day. Even when you don't want to get out of bed, when you're not in the right mood, when it would be so much easier to just "mail it in." Take it from someone who spent some time earlier in his career mailing it in. It's not worth it. The hard way makes the journey that much better. Learning to give your best even when you don't have your best is the mark of a true professional. You owe this to yourself.

This is what builds character. This is what makes you stronger.

This commitment and effort literally does more for your continued development and evolution than anything else. We don't admire this consistency and longevity enough in business. We're always looking for the big bang. But what do we do when we're not firing on all cylinders? Like a baseball pitcher without his best fastball, you have to dig into your arsenal and see what else you have. Find those secondary *pitches*—those "little things" that will make a difference.

Be willing to find a way, to keep moving forward when you don't have it, when you're hurting for confidence and doubting yourself. To get to where you really want to be, you'll get there faster when you do your best each day, even when everything is telling you to give in to the path of least resistance. That's pro.

You have to know a cold, hard truth: we're all going to get knocked on our asses at some point or another, whether we see it coming or not. That's not a maybe, that's a definite. For you, as a champion leader, it's not a matter of if you'll get up but how quickly and how prepared you will become for the next moment. That's how you build resilience. This is the mindset of a champion—when you refuse to accept permanent defeat and commit to trying again and again.

Chapter 11

Leadership Heart 'n' Soul (*Learn to Lead with Compassion and Spirit*)

"Good teams become great ones when the members trust each other enough to surrender the Me for the We."

—Phil Jackson

Few leaders have ever attained the team success that Hall of Fame basketball coach Phil Jackson did during his coaching tenure in the National Basketball Association (NBA). The soul of Jackson's team success was recognizing that talent alone would not win championships. Rather, it would take bringing people together and getting them to sacrifice personal glories for the betterment of the team. Jackson learned throughout a remarkable basketball life that each individual's contributions held unique value to the organization.

Phil Jackson was like the music director of a symphony orchestra—able to bring incredibly talented people together to produce their best music. He didn't just "roll out the ball" and sit on the sidelines with his arms crossed. He established vision and invited his players to view it with him. Jackson's championship leadership empowered every player to think for themselves and play instinctively by providing a well-defined structure for how to operate. This structure became known as the "Triangle Offense" and it was the foundation for the 11 NBA championships that his teams won.

Know this: It took Michael Jordan until his seventh full season in the NBA to win a title. Kobe Bryant came together with Shaquille

O'Neal, who was entering his eighth full season, to win their first championship. This all happened under Jackson's tutelage. And it's no coincidence. It's a lesson that even superstars—or the rock stars we're accustomed to hearing about in organizations—cannot do it on their own. It's championship leadership that brings talented people together and gets them to subordinate individual success for team achievement. As the African proverb says, "If you want to go fast, go alone. If you want to go far, go together."

Jackson's Triangle Offense gave each player the latitude and purpose to continually create opportunities for one another. It entrusted as much responsibility in the star players as it did in the role players and secondary contributors. It was basketball (and team-building) genius and it helped each player fully actualize their potential.

As Jackson said in his book *Eleven Rings: The Soul of Success*, "As a leader, your job is to do everything in your power to create the perfect conditions for success by benching your ego and inspiring your team to play the game the right way. But at some point, you need to let go. . . . The soul of success is surrendering to what is."[1]

He challenged each player to grow as a person first—recommending books and outlets for self-awareness and personal development. He famously gifted *Siddhartha*, a book about self-discovery, to Shaq. He emphasized spiritual and mental wellness and growth. Jackson introduced mindfulness meditation to his players during training camp and led them through mindfulness sessions before practices and games. He'd have the players assemble around half-court and meditate together. They visualized themselves on the court, seeing the game play out in their minds. It calmed their nerves and gave them the collective chemistry and mental preparation to go out and win.

Jackson always made a point to deliver key messages privately to players in one-on-one conversations because he knew individualizing his message to each person would build trust and understanding.

These one-on-one conversations featured learning, skill building, and conceptual understanding of how the Bulls and Lakers teams would execute on the basketball court. He saw this not as a "nice to have" but as a necessary supplement to long-term individual growth.

But the brilliance of Jackson was so much more than just "X's and O's." Jackson's spiritual side, aided by his Zen Buddhist learnings and practices, helped him bring each organization together to care about one another.

He knew the players' subject and functional knowledge alone wouldn't suffice. To come together as a team and better understand one another, they needed to better understand themselves. Jackson helped them figure this out for themselves. He knew micromanagement wouldn't work. His players praised him for it. His teams always had the mental and emotional clarity on the court to perform at a high level. From there, muscle memory and skill would take over during tense moments in games.

Are you seeing the parallels here to how you can connect with your team?

Whether on the basketball hardwood, an innovation lab, the boardroom, or the manufacturing floor, as a leader you can impart the lessons of hard work and selflessness. As you form closer bonds with your team, implore both individual contributors and fellow leaders to speak up and carry this message. You want your words and actions to replenish and reinforce one another and to unify the team to achieve the organizational mission. The ideal state is to have such a close connection and shared belief with your senior leaders and top performers that they become your "eyes and ears" while delivering the work.

This all begins way before you start executing and working on strategic initiatives together. It's the effort made to empathize and communicate with your people—to understand who they are and to gather their input to form a championship organization.

Inspirational Leadership

To become inspirational and influential as a leader, you're going to want to find your "rocks" and "champions" to lean on and help to catalyze others. Inspirational leaders share the victories, setbacks, and lessons they've learned from their own and other people's stories. They possess what I like to call "CHG"—the courage to always do the right thing, humility to give credit to others, and gratitude to express a kind "thank you for your contributions." Inspirational leadership ignites the fire inside of us, giving us the energy and motivation to lead people with passion. It awakens the positive emotions that bring people together around a vision of hope and potential for the future. I encourage you to inspire each person around you to recognize their own unique strengths, value, and potential contributions to the success of the team.

Inspiring leaders channel their emotions, creating a positive energy surge that boosts employee performance. It is because of this united optimism, vision, and unshakeable conviction that your team will succeed. It's what we saw in Lisa Su's incredible success story at AMD and learned through Indra Nooyi's sage guidance.

Inspirational leadership means that you're going to over-communicate and work to over-deliver. Make sure you understand your clients' and employees' needs and wants and that your people understand what you're delivering for them. The same goes for you, making sure everything you communicate is understood and acknowledged. Be in the business of listening. Be known as empathetic and results-driven in your approach, and in how you build relationships and achieve results.

Let's see what inspirational leadership isn't:

- **It's *not* talking behind each other's backs:** Loose lips sink ships. In order to stick together, it's critical to unify through the importance of the goals you're looking to achieve, the clients you're aiming to retain, and the new clients you're looking to add.

- **It's *not* looking back:** Instead, focus on the present (clients you're serving today and what you're doing for them) and the future (how you're influencing and appealing to the clients you want to have). This takes strategic thinking and it's something you must build in, as individuals, each day to make sure you're always innovating and anticipating.
- **It's *not* doing things on your own:** There needs to be collaboration and clear communication in *all* that you do. Don't operate in a vacuum—connect and be proactive in how you communicate. It's through speaking up and finding time to connect that you let others know how to support you, so you have what you need to be successful.

Going Back to Your Roots

Northwestern University defines spiritual wellness as "expanding a sense of purpose and meaning in life, including one's morals and ethics."[2] The more we understand our spiritual side as leaders, the inner-working of what makes us who we are, the greater chance we have at finding equanimity. We can give this gift to others.

We may expect a lot of ourselves, which comes through setting objectives and goals, but that's not the same as putting unnecessary pressure on ourselves to perform. Pressure is increased when we procrastinate and find outlets to use up our time on activities that don't match our plans. Pressure also comes when we set unrealistic goals.

Next time you find yourself getting off track, get back to your roots. Get back to your values, as we learned in Chapter 2. Remind yourself of your core values and beliefs—those that breathe life into you and make you tick. Act on those qualities and allow them to transform your mind and renew your purpose. There's always an opportunity for us to revisit the foundation of what makes us who we are. When we're living in alignment with our values and inspiring others, we're living a life of integrity.

Tying Your Character to Your Organization's Identity

Just like your character becomes your identity, the identity of your team and organization are how people come to know your culture. Character and identity are consciously chosen. It's critical to tap into the spiritual side of your identity to find that wellspring of leadership DNA that makes you, you. Aligning your thoughts, words, and actions together gives you clarity and self-awareness that help you to show up in the exact way that you want to see yourself at your best. You can accomplish this through a consistent journaling and self-feedback process. Build in time each evening for 5–10 minutes to process your thoughts. Is the way you really feel how you're speaking and showing up with your team?

Tjada D'Oyen McKenna is the CEO of Mercy Corps and the only Black woman in charge of a major American humanitarian organization. Mercy Corps "seek solutions to the world's toughest challenges. To take on the consequences of conflict and climate change, we bring together bold ideas and the lived experience of people who know their communities best—scaling what works to achieve lasting, transformational change."[3]

D'oyen McKenna's inspirational leadership has helped the organization grow by making sure their communities are well served. She said, "I want Mercy Corps to be a place where you can grow. . . . No matter where people live, we need to provide people with opportunities to self-actualize."[4]

She's spoken about how much it means to members of the communities they serve to see a Black female in a leadership position. It gives them strength, inspiration, and hope. It also inspires fellow members of the organization. It cannot be understated just how much this matters to members of minority communities. I see it locally in the tri-county area of Charleston, South Carolina, with my wife, Tosha Connors, and the organization she leads, My Sister's House. As a biracial woman, her visibility to the many Black constituents they serve strikes a powerful chord. It also shows the organization's female employees a powerful example of a woman of color leading with class and integrity.

Inspiration is created when we see someone like us accomplishing the things that we aspire to achieve.

Finding the Leader Within

I'm always surprised when champion leaders tell me they never envisioned or saw themselves in a position to want to lead or manage people. They genuinely loved the work they were doing earlier in their careers, as individual contributors, and took a lot of pride as the subject matter expert and sought-after person in that niche. The truth is, it's very hard to give that up. We don't want to let go of the work that's given us the credibility and respect that we've earned. Finding the leader within often places us at a decision point where we need to evaluate our desire to lead versus our ability to influence as an individual contributor.

As stated by Molly Graham in the article "'Give Away Your Legos' and Other Commandments for Scaling Startups":

> The emotions you feel when new people are coming in and taking over pieces of your job—it's not that different from how a kid feels when they have to share their Legos. There's a lot of natural anxiety and insecurity that the new person won't build your Lego tower in the right way, or

> that they'll get to take all the fun or important Legos, or that if they take over the part of the Lego tower you were building, then there won't be any Legos left for you.[5]

Don't be afraid to let go of one thing in order to gain more of something else. Many managers and leaders that I coach each week tell me that they enjoy being able to influence larger scopes of work and reach more people. There's always a trade-off. I've found that most people, who take that next step to leadership, were inspired by the mentorship of their own leader and genuinely loved the way they were treated. Iron sharpens iron!

Many leaders realize they can only build, do, or accomplish so much without a team behind them. The wisdom of the African proverb earlier reminds us that we can accomplish tremendous things working together as a team. Even as an individual contributor, you need to be able to communicate complex ideas and get buy-in from team members to advance them. There's a collaborative element to the work that we do in organizations. You have the ability to influence that, regardless of your role, every day.

Questions for reflection:

- Who do you look to as the people you can lean on most to drive things to get done?
- What are some ways you can get in touch with your spiritual side as a leader?
- How can you integrate inspirational leadership qualities into your own leadership style?
- What part of your leadership "DNA" do you most want to show in how you lead others?

The Human Element

When we look across industries, whether it's automobile manufacturing and a people-first leader such as Alan Mulally, or women's fashion and a trailblazer such as Sara Blakely, the human element is a uniting thread of the champion leader. And yet, this heart 'n' soul isn't so easy to find in the digital, data-driven world that we live in.

You can have a sharp business acumen and proven experience at delivering results, but if you lack the ability to connect and bring people together for a common mission, you will not succeed at building high-performing teams in the long run. If you only ever make time for work and ignore relationships, you will create a gulf between yourself and the people you need to collaborate with. We're at a point in history where we may have the most educated, high IQ workforce, but it's EQ that's needed for a connected workforce.

Subject and functional matter expertise matter a lot. We see it with a strategic and tactical encyclopedia of American football knowledge such as Kansas City Chiefs head coach Andy Reid. He knows the game as well as any coach in history. He's forever changed the way offensive football is played. But it's the human element of connection that he's created that makes players want to play for him. The powerful relationship that he's built with three-time Super Bowl MVP quarterback Patrick Mahomes is palpable. Both men are talented and gifted as coach and athlete. But it's been Reid's ability to connect with Mahomes and let him be, well, himself.

Mahomes said, "He's meant the world to me. He's . . . one of the best coaches of all time, but he's just one of the best people of all time. He's learned how to get the most out of me every day. He doesn't let me be satisfied with where I'm at. He teaches me a ton. Not only the quarterback position, but how to be a leader and how to be a great dad and how to be a great husband. He lets me be who I am every single day."[6]

Mahomes's words are a powerful testament to how you can teach and coach someone, while still allowing them to be uniquely themselves.

I think about how the human element shows up in my own life. The incredible love I have for my boys and wife makes me smile and fills me up with joy. It inspires me and influences my work. When people talk about the most important things in life, that's what I think of. People. When you can smile at someone because you're thrilled to see them? That's a special, electric feeling. That's how I feel when I see clients and businesses that I'm ecstatic to collaborate with. I want to share in that joy with presence and clear eyes.

If you genuinely want to help someone, lead with honesty, energy, and authenticity. If you tell someone the truth but do it without any real care that lets the person know you're trying to help them, then your message will fall flat. They might hear your words, but they're not really listening to what you say. Speak the truth, and always be accountable to your word. Lead with positive energy that brightens someone's mood and elevates them to want to do great work. Charge your battery each day! Don't give people the final 15% juice of your smartphone battery. Replenish yourself, and give them 100% of yourself.

I've found over and over again, if you're willing to be authentic and help people, people will let you help them. They'll partner with you and do great work. They'll elevate the culture of your organization to create belonging.

That's real. This is all born from embracing a mindset that seeks to provide the truth. It's focused on growth and relationship building that forms connection.

Heart 'n' Soul

What makes up the heart and soul of a high-performing team?

As we've learned, it's a well-rounded package of tangibles and intangibles. There are mental, emotional, social, and spiritual elements that constitute the core of every great team. You need recruiting and human resources to find the talent—to help fit your organization with the people who will make it great. You want to find people who have skills, positive attitudes, and hard-work ethics that believe in "the power of team" more than they do "the power of me."

Having advanced analytics and data to find the right people has become an essential part of every organization's people strategy. Once you've onboarded new team members, it's critical for each individual to understand their role on the team, and to "know thyself," as it relates to mastering self-awareness. Building relationships and learning how to influence and adapt in a new organizational culture gives someone a baseline for making an impact.

In the modern workplace, there's a lack of social skills and a certain level of awkwardness that some employees feel around assimilating and bonding with their teammates, fellow employees, and customers. I encourage you to keep things loose and simple. Be guided by getting to know people as human beings first. Educate and train your employees on the virtues and values of emotional intelligence, while improving their social environments to be ones that are conducive to acceptance and empathy.

The time investment is negligible in the long term and the upfront financial cost is minuscule when compared to what it costs to replace an employee who leaves your organization. Emotional intelligence is so integral to the rhythm of frontline day-to-day performance (at the micro-level), but it's equally important at the operational level for how teams treat all of their personnel.

Every high-performing team builds from the ground up around camaraderie, chemistry, and teamwork. They cut no corners and operate with maximum efficiency that's paired by an emotionally intelligent touch.

Do You Have a "Have"?

For a long time, we've been fed a be-do-have system of thinking on success. It all culminates in a bottom-line approach and a "What have you done for me lately?" vibe. When this happens inside an organization, it can negatively affect the way people treat one another. What happens when the getting isn't good? If you're only focused on results, you risk harming relationships by playing a game that's virtually impossible to win in the long term. No one is saying you shouldn't be results-focused. Always strive to achieve the best results. But I encourage you to reframe how you see the "have" part of things from both a team and individual perspective.

This is a call to recognize that people's needs, self-care, and emotional self-regulation matter—including our own. This isn't a fluffy, fanciful thought; it's what the best leaders in the world understand and take into account each day. Ask yourself, "What is my *have* feeling?" What do you need to feel emotionally fulfilled and sustained? If you see yourself as having this already, it shifts the way you approach each day. I encourage you to go deeper and think about this and help your team members to identify their own *have*. It will make the *do* and *be* parts much easier.

Owning Up to Failures

If you've ever failed at anything in your life, you know that the hardest part of recovering is coming to grips with reality. It's admitting to yourself that you fell short—no matter how shell-shocked you are in the moment. It's accepting defeat, no matter how much it stings.

Even though we know everyone makes mistakes, it feels different when it's *us*. We may easily bestow grace and encouragement to someone else, but we can have a hard time forgiving ourselves. Let me boldly tell you: stop the self-blame game. And certainly, don't seek to blame others. It will get you nowhere. **Own it.**

Own your shortcomings and move forward with professionalism and integrity. Failure is not the end. It's temporary. Failure is not where we should get lost in fear. No one likes to talk about their most intimate personal or professional failures in the moment because they're embarrassed. They're confused. It hurts. They're lacking self-awareness because it feels like their world is, at least temporarily, caving in.

In *Toughness*, Jay Bilas wrote, "Failing doesn't make you a failure. Failing makes you a competitor. Every competitor fails. If you lay it on the line, you will come up short at times. Failure is a part of competing, and embracing that fact is an important component of toughness. Tough people fail, but tough people are not failures. The only failures are those who give up, or give in."[7]

Champion leaders also have to deal with owning up to failures on a team level. Part of it is having an accepting mindset that it could happen, and if it does, that you'll profit from it and push forward with greater resilience. It's part of the wild, roller-coaster ride of Nike's rise to success as detailed brilliantly by Phil Knight in *Shoe Dog*. Knight wrote, "Fear of failure, I thought, will never be our downfall as a company. Not that any of us thought we wouldn't fail; in fact, we had every expectation that we would. But when we did fail, we had faith that we'd do it fast, learn from it, and be better for it."[8]

You lose when you don't learn or grow from mistakes. You win when you realize failure is really a friend. You win when you appreciate the wealth of information gained, the clarity revealed, and the lessons that propel you to your next triumph. It all begins with acceptance. Things turn around when you start to see the positive. Shawn Achor writes in *The Happiness Advantage*, "Constantly scanning the world for the negative comes with a great cost. It undercuts our creativity, raises our stress levels, and lowers our motivation and ability to accomplish goals."[9]

During moments of difficulty, these words from my dad have always stuck with me: "Things will work out. They always do."

Throughout my life, I've found comfort in those words. I've used them to build optimism, belief, and hope that has provided me with self-assuredness to keep going. This encourages confidence, perseverance, and an attitude of expectancy that recharges our battery, empowering and centering us.

In Closing

English novelist Rudyard Kipling wrote in *The Jungle Book*, "For the strength of the pack is the wolf, and the strength of the wolf is the pack."[10]

As you think about your team, remember to deeply value each individual's contributions. Lead them, teach them, coach them, and correct them when you need to. But also, allow them to be themselves. Good teams have good performers. Championship teams have top-notch performers who always seek to make the team better. We before me. That's the real strength of the pack. And it's the heart 'n' soul of leadership.

Leadership Heart 'n' Soul Exercise

Ask each team member to reflect on their personal and professional identity. Give them a set period of time—maybe two weeks or one month. Encourage them to journal thoughts and capture ideas over time. Ask them to list out the qualities and pieces of their character that make them uniquely themselves. Then, see what synchronization there is between their personal and professional lives.

The goal is to see how each person shows up at work and home and how similar their identities are. Do this for yourself. See how your authenticity and true character shines through. Come together and share your results. You can do this in a one-on-one or team environment, your choice. Ask people what they feel most comfortable with. If you choose to share in a team setting, create a psychologically safe environment for doing so.

Champion's Checklist (Tools and Takeaways)

☑ Carry over courage, humility, and gratitude (CHG) to your team conversations.

☑ Highlight and praise the character and identity of your team.

☑ Integrate the human element into every relationship you have, and keep it top of mind.

☑ Always tell the truth.

☑ When it comes to failure and mistakes, be a lifelong student. Understand what went wrong, and gain wisdom from each experience.

Chapter 12

The Drive for More (*Guide Your Team to Always Move Forward*)

"Somehow I can't believe that there are any heights that can't be scaled by a man who knows the secrets of making dreams come true. This special secret, it seems to me, can be summarized in four Cs. They are curiosity, confidence, courage, and constancy, and the greatest of all is confidence. When you believe in a thing, believe in it all the way, implicitly and unquestionably"

—Walt Disney

Every year, there's a new Major League Baseball opening day. A time of optimism. A time where maybe, just maybe, this is *your* team's year. The teams, players, and fans all start with a blank slate. As the saying goes: hope springs eternal. Late March/early April coincides with the season of renewal, spring. A fresh, new beginning and hope are in the air. I've found both the dawn—and the rhythm—of a baseball season can mirror our daily lives. Allow me to explain.

We can renew our minds and see each new day as an opportunity to make a huge difference in our own lives, as well as our customers' and employees' lives. Each day we can make micro-gains that help us to form winning habits. Our daily dedication to our work comes back to discipline, consistency, motivation, and professionalism. When we apply these keys to success, great things begin to happen. Even in the face of adversity.

Have a bad day? There's always the opportunity to go out and have a *great* one tomorrow. Hey, maybe the first part of your day didn't get off to a good start. There's an opportunity for renewal to make the second half better. Take your foot off the gas, pump the brakes a bit, and give yourself a personal reset. You have this power to stop, reflect, and think positively.

Have a great day? Excellent! Keep building on it. But remember, past performance does not guarantee future results. Humbling? Yes. Also, a call to approach each day—and each moment—with humility, focus, hard work, and positive energy.

The leaders that I've coached and worked with who find the most success and happiness are the ones who've built a foundation on values, defined purpose, and goals. They consistently pursue each new day with confidence, courage, and optimism.

Some days, you will succeed. Other days, you won't. Many of the greatest baseball players to ever wear a uniform struck out—*a lot.* Even the best hitters in the game do not get a hit—nor reach base—the majority of the time. Think about that. Simply put—they do not succeed. What I've always deeply admired about their professionalism and drive for more is their willingness to put the past behind them and live in the present moment with belief—to trust their plan.

Former Major League Baseball player Tony Gwynn was one of the greatest hitters to ever live. He succeeded as a hitter about as often as any player in the history of the game. He said, "The first part about being a good hitter, before you even get in the batter's box, is number one, mentally, you gotta believe that 'hey, I can have success.' And how you have success—how you have consistent success—is by being consistent with your approach."[1]

That approach—that mindset and daily routine—is something that all of us can make our own. It's having unwavering perseverance in the face of failure. The willingness to try again, and believe that things will be better next time. It's not getting too high—or too low—based on our results. It's refusing to give up when things don't break your way.

Baseball players learn a new insight from each walk-up to the plate. Each pitch taken. Each opportunity to look the pitcher in the eye, reassure themselves, and approach the next pitch with belief and confidence. This is the mindset of elite baseball players, but it's also the mindset of champion leaders.

I encourage you to find comfort in knowing that success comes when you keep going and persevere, even when you haven't yet seen the fruits of your labor.

You won't always achieve a positive result. Many of the seeds that you sow as a champion leader take time to sprout. Keep going. Work hard and give your best each day for yourself, for the people you lead and for your organization. When you're optimistic, you'll always learn. When you learn, you'll remain curious, and when you're curious you'll find new ways to succeed. You'll find fulfillment in your work. Here's to new beginnings.

Take Your Time and Build Trust

There's a tremendous amount of cynicism in modern business.

Employees are struggling to trust their leaders. They're skeptical of the direction their organizations are headed in. It mirrors the distrust that many people have in the media, politicians, and some institutions. When this happens, a divide is created. Where division reigns, distrust rears its head. And as we know, the most important part of leadership is building trust with the people you lead. Without it, nothing else matters.

Leading from a position of trust, you have the guiding core values of authenticity, integrity, and honesty to serve as the checkpoints for every word you say and every decision you make. One of Coach John Wooden's maxims is "Be quick, don't hurry." Remember to pace yourself and take time to establish trust with your team. Follow through on your words—this cannot be emphasized enough. It's how you create strong bonds. Fractured relationships are very challenging to heal. It's why assuming positive intent, and always being conscientious of leading this way, will create equity with everyone. When your team knows that you're all-in, camaraderie begins to grow.

The intuition and attitude that we carry into every interaction factors into the way we communicate, identify opportunities, build relationships, and make intelligent, smart decisions. How we recharge and champion ourselves positively influences our self-awareness and helps us to lead at our best. It's this optimal level of mindset and action that we strive for and aim to mobilize for our teams.

Be Proactive

Your passion and understanding for how to influence every new client, customer, and stakeholder will help you build a dynamic and emotionally intelligent culture in your organization. It begins with you and how you motivate and inspire yourself each day. This drive feels empowering and reinvigorating. This helps you create as much impact as possible. As we discussed in Chapter 10, the best leaders obsess over the small details and "little things" because they know those things are exactly what leads to big results for customers and employees alike.

Be proactive, not reactive. Don't just let things happen. Make them happen. Having a proactive mindset means that you:

- Initiate contact first; seek to establish relationships. Proactively follow up and maintain each relationship you have;
- Stay aware of threats and disruptions to your business by managing risks;

- Dedicate resources to training and development for your teams; and
- Encourage everyone in your organization to speak up, share ideas, and take actions.

By doing these things, you place your organization and team in a position to anticipate people's needs.

One other important part of staying proactive is recognizing that there is an inherently political aspect to almost every job. It's true. That doesn't mean we have to be *political*, but that we're astutely aware of our surroundings. Think wisely before you say and do things. Be yourself, be inclusive, and don't get caught up in "playing politics," which means wasting time on the petty, fruitless things. The perfect example is never to speak poorly of someone behind their backs. Avoid gossip, and act with integrity. Think first, before you act.

Remember the wisdom of the Eisenhower decision-making matrix. Leave the unimportant and nonurgent things in the trash bin. Champion leaders don't have time for politics. Focus instead on getting people on board with your vision to ensure everyone in your organization is rowing in the same direction. Spending quality time together and communicating proactively will be your biggest competitive advantages.

External Validation and Internal Validation

You do not need to be validated by others in order to feel that you're succeeding. Flip it around. Remember the "have" mindset from Chapter 11. Start with internal validation.

External validation is nice, but we should never feel we *need* this to legitimize who we are. Our own thoughts, ideas, accomplishments, and actions do that. External validation adds to the growing number of voices that believe in what we do. But it doesn't define us.

A "reward" or external validation doesn't compare to knowing you've achieved success on your terms. True success comes from the inside. It's born from great opportunity, which is only recognized and conquered once we are truly prepared for it—once we're ready for it. And guess what. I think we're all a lot more *ready* for the biggest opportunities and moments in our lives than we may realize. Focus on the moment. Embrace it. Focus on what success means to you. Take the time to speak it out loud and write it down. This means committing to a goal, building a plan to achieve it, and immersing yourself in the experience to the maximum degree. Then, you'll know you've achieved success on your terms. You'll understand the extraordinary power of internal validation.

Questions for reflection:

- Ask yourself, How can I clearly and concisely communicate my standard of performance to others so they understand it?
- What changes would you like to make to your approach and daily routine?
- What can you do for yourself when it comes to internal validation?
- What pieces of external validation and recognition are most important to you?

Imagine What Could Be

When I was a kid, it was a special treat to have birthday parties at McDonald's. They created such memorable characters that made you smile. When we were there, we could live in this imaginary world where a Hamburglar and a large purple creature named, Grimace, could talk to us. What Ray Kroc and his business associates really created at their restaurants was an *experience*. An experience that all of us wanted to be a part of because it felt special and rewarding.

When we think about the organizations and people who have inspired us and captivated our attention, it often comes back to creative imagination. It comes back to feeling like a kid again and wanting to have fun.

Somewhere along the way we stopped thinking work was fun, and we stopped trying to find more fun moments throughout the day. The notion that "work is fun!" became too contrived or hard to believe, for some. As the leader, you have enormous ability to influence the fun that your team has. Maybe it's time to look inward and think about how you can bring your authentic self to work each day and make things more enjoyable. Whether that's awarding a "Championship belt" or trophy to a team member for acts of kindness in a given month, or heck, maybe even handing out a McDonald's Happy Meal toy for an important contribution, feel free to tinker around, and have fun with having fun!

Find the Path Forward

If you ever dare to believe that motivation isn't real, then it's worth asking yourself: "What truly drives me to do what I do each day?" It's a question worth asking every business day of your life—one that I got in the habit of asking myself when I found discontent and felt let down.

It's part of my own story of feeling that I didn't have a champion leader to partner with me to drive my own career. I landed a fantastic management consulting job out of graduate school, one that paid well and offered great benefits and prestige—and I believed, a fast track to the top of the business world. I got to work with top organizations and clients—I felt *limitless*, like Bradley Cooper's character from the film.

I also realized I didn't know exactly what each next step would look like. I've found this to be common for most people I've met throughout my life and business journey. It's part of the fun, yet also part of the challenge of knowing who and what we want to be. It's harder to advance our careers when we don't have someone championing our development. As I looked around earlier in my career, I saw colleagues who had caring leaders that helped guide their career development as they advanced upward in the organization. Those who didn't have champion leaders often left for new opportunities.

The influence of a champion leader, someone who knows the art of asking questions and delivering timely, profound messages, helps create vision and infuses fun. It provokes thought and illuminates that path forward for us to light the way and figure out on our own terms exactly what we want for our careers. Do we want to influence the lives of people? Do we want to create a new technology, and in the words of Steve Jobs, "Put 1,000 songs in your pocket," or do we want to blaze a path for creating wealth for others and bringing them stability and peace of mind?

There's nothing more spectacular than someone believing in you and sticking with you throughout your entire journey to help you become who you've always wanted to be. The champion leader humanizes the leadership conversation with love, fun, heart, tenacity, and a joie de vivre that people want to embrace. This is an equal opportunity skill set. All of us can do this for someone else.

What We All Value

We shouldn't just hope for the help of others to advance our careers. Think about it, we don't just hope for someone else to come along and become our friend or life partner. We need to partner with others and make things happen. We have an innate human craving for positive social interactions. Don't believe me? Take this from neuroscientists at MIT:

> People who are forced to be isolated crave social interactions similarly to the way a hungry person craves food. Our finding fits the intuitive idea that positive social interactions are a basic human need, and acute loneliness is an aversive state that motivates people to repair what is lacking, similar to hunger.[2]

We want to be happy. But in order for us to be both successful and happy, we need to recognize that the same people willing to help us are also looking for the exact same thing for themselves.

And why wouldn't they? Isn't that what we're trying to do? So how do we get people to take an interest in us—to help us achieve our big goals and purpose? We respond by taking an active interest in helping others back. We don't just do it as an obligation or because we *think* it's the right thing to do. We make an active choice to become personally invested in another person's success and happiness. This innate desire to help is what builds connection and belonging!

That investment of time is always time well spent. It has a compounding effect that helps elevate us in our own pursuits. In a constantly evolving world, we have to look out for ourselves and recognize what we need to do to preserve our self-interest. An emotionally intelligent leader is interested in overall success and achievement—not just for themselves but for their peers. Their inspired leadership and passion, combined with their optimism, drives them to want to be their best for themselves *and* others.

What I've observed on the front lines of leadership and management conversations is that employers deeply value a workforce with highly emotionally intelligent individuals. I'm told very frequently some version of "I can teach the hard skills, but I want to hire people with high character who have soft skills." Soft skills such as the ability to communicate, lead others, and be empathetic toward their colleagues.

If you have a game plan for your own success, chances are you can help someone else with theirs. If you have the ability, it's a matter of generating the desire. Sometimes, it's best to reverse-engineer from what success looks like, to help us develop our game plan, which is initially fueled by our passion and desire. Take this as observed by the Greater Good Science Center at UC Berkeley:

> A recent article published in *The Journal of Positive Psychology* by Daryl Van Tongeren and his colleagues sought to examine this relationship [how kindness and happiness help us find purpose]. In a preliminary study, the researchers asked over 400 participants to report on how frequently they engage in different altruistic behaviors (such as volunteering) and how meaningful their life feels. Participants who were more altruistic reported a greater sense of purpose and meaning in their lives.[4,5]

Wouldn't you want to have a greater sense of meaning and purpose in your life? Wouldn't you agree that once you do, it's that much easier to be successful?

We want to know and feel that we're making an impact. We also want to know how we've done. We want to receive feedback and feel appreciated, validated, recognized, encouraged, motivated, inspired, directed, and guided to the next opportunity.

At the close of the Beatles' famous London rooftop concert in January of 1969, John Lennon is heard saying, "I hope we've passed the audition," in a sarcastic manner. But nevertheless, even one of the most influential, successful figures in the history of music, finished with a reflective aim at approval. Did he need it? Of course not.

But, this validation helps us to know we're on the right track. Even when we *know* we are moving in the right direction. Even when we've validated that for ourselves. It's OK to seek this approval. This is part of what drives us forward.

Hold Yourself to a High Standard

Never compromise your standard. Never. This may seem intransigent or stubborn, but it's actually one of the most important qualities to have in leadership. By holding yourself and others accountable to a clear and attainable standard, provided through vision, mission, and goals, you are delivering the structure necessary to allow your organization to be successful. Manage people and adapt to people, but don't second-guess yourself on holding yourself to a high standard.

What worked for someone else may not work for you. The fun part is figuring out what *will* work for you. Success isn't linear, nor can you plan for every step of the journey without needing to improvise. There are a lot of starts, stops, squiggles, shimmies, and steps backward on the path forward. The most exciting part of building a high-performing team is determining what ingredients you need for success, fulfillment, and happiness both today and going forward.

You as a leader get to be the architect and builder of that. By putting into action your strategy, you are actively working each day toward building habits to achieve goals that will drive your team forward. Keep refining your plan. Reflect. Use self-awareness for growth and understand what it means to adapt when things aren't working. Always learn. Always grow. And never lower your standard. Holding yourself and your team to a high standard is what makes you great.

Run Your Own Race

As a leader, it's imperative to use competitive energy to help you focus to do your best.

It's truly about immersing yourself in what you're doing and getting "in the zone" in an effort to be your best. If you're looking to build an app, does it really matter whether you know or don't know if someone else is trying to create a similar app? I believe that answer is a resounding no. Timing may matter in some instances, but the best product always wins. There's always room for another innovation and outstanding entry to the market.

The best effort, combined with your natural talents, skills, goals, purpose, and mission, is indestructible and all-powerful. When you're trying to reach that VP job at your marketing agency, financial services firm, or law firm, it's about you and not them. Incredibly, so many of us fail to understand this. We waste time comparing ourselves to others, when the only comparative analysis we need is to measure our progress against becoming the best version of ourselves we should want to be. Comparison really is the thief of joy.

Set goals. Set the bar very high. But don't shift these things around for what you perceive others to be doing. This breeds envy, and envy converts itself into frustration, anger, jealousy, hatred, and even laziness. Envy seems like it's a convertible energy for good, at first blush. But it always ends badly. Run your own race.

Forecasting the Need for Championship Leadership

In 2011, CareerBuilder ran a survey that showed a whopping 71% of employers said they valued emotional intelligence more than IQ.[6] Over 13 years later, in my conversations with C-suite leaders, executives, and managers, I estimate that number to be even higher.

In fact, in 2019: "Research conducted with Fortune 500 CEOs by the Stanford Research Institute International and the Carnegie Mellon Foundation, found that 75% of long-term job success depends on people skills, while only 25% on technical knowledge."[7]

More and more organizations will continue to look for leaders that possess people skills and the ability to connect with their employees. This all begins with having a positive attitude, desire, and commitment to helping people.

Jack Zenger and Joseph Folkman write in *Harvard Business Review* that their "examination of 360-degree assessment data from more than 60,000 leaders showed us that leaders who were rated in the top quartile of both skills [business results and people skills] ranked in the 91st percentile of all leaders . . . the best leaders are the very ones who manage to do both."[8]

They go on to point out that "older or more powerful managers would also benefit from emphasizing their people skills, even if they don't realize it."

Championship leadership isn't a skill set that's limited to younger managers or a particular generation of leaders. There isn't a time or age limit on when this need for people skills and social connection expires. The drive for more means positioning yourself for the long game by building relationships and leading with conviction. This conviction is backed by a values and belief system that will sustain you throughout it all.

Remember this—you're doing a disservice to the people around you by not giving them the gift of championship leadership. You have it in you. Don't worry about saving it up for another day—focus on helping someone now.

I try to stay out of the business of predictions and pop cultural observations. When I was younger, after seeing the movie *Back to the Future Part II,* I boldly predicted that every child would soon have their own hover board. OK. Not quite yet. But there's still hope! Until recently, I thought Bad Bunny was the fairytale villain in the Disney movie my three-year old was watching. See what I mean? I'm not always accurate!

But if there's one thing that I feel very confident in forecasting, it's the need for caring, assertive, thoughtful leaders who will be able to adapt to a rapidly evolving technological landscape. The foundation of high-performing teams is emotional intelligence, camaraderie, and communication that provides understanding and direction. While I may have been wrong about hover boards, I'm as sure about the foundation of high-performing teams as I am that the sun will rise in the east tomorrow morning.

Keep It Simple . . .

We're more inundated than ever with choices, options, and thousands of things to choose from. Look at the number of television and entertainment subscription services there are now: Prime, Hulu, Netflix, Disney+, Plus +, Plus -, Minus +. OK, I made those last few up. But the point is, it's become absurd. How could we keep track? It's always best to keep things simple. Think about it, the most memorable music over the years is often crafted from the simplest chords and lyrics. The most memorable leadership is crafted from simple words, intentions, and actions.

I encourage you on your drive forward to use this simple success formula for champion leaders: ***Positive attitude + Imagination + Hard work + Perseverance = Success.***

You can print this out and look at it each day or week to make sure you're staying true to who you are. You don't have to outthink yourself. Keep it simple in your approach, and trust that the foundation this book has helped you to establish will lead you to many daily victories.

. . . And Keep the Faith

Dr. Jeremy E. Sherman writes in *Psychology Today*:

> We work from the evidence at hand to [place] confidence in a bet we think will work. And work is the point of faith: Only so many hours in the day and we don't use them just for wondering, but for doing focused work. Since most things take concerted effort and time, we need to focus. Focused work is concentrated work, work based on consistent bets on what will work.[9]

I like to think of this as small bets—small, continuous bets of faith in ourselves and the people around us. The key is to have faith, even when you don't immediately see the rewards of your hard work. Find a mental and emotional target that you can believe in. Continue pushing forward when you haven't yet seen the fruits of your labor.

Championship leadership is about being the best we can for ourselves and being the best we can for the people we lead. This means gaining self-awareness, which helps us better understand ourselves and how to support our teams. It's using motivation and inspiration to generate passion and belief in our team. This helps us solve problems and execute at a high level. It leads to the development of people.

We grow and gain momentum by emulating role models that resonate with us. These are the people—a step or two ahead of us, no matter their title—who show us what success can look like for ourselves. We can then imagine it and build a plan to achieve it. It's this perseverance that leads us to always want to improve—to always strive toward something bigger, better, and bolder than who we currently are.

I encourage you to keep what's most important at the forefront of your life. Your relationship with yourself, your family, friends, colleagues, and partners. It's people that matter. By doing this, you will keep yourself centered. By keeping the faith that you're doing the right things, you will avoid putting too much pressure on yourself. Yes, people are counting on you. But when you accept that as a rewarding, competitive challenge and not a burden or feeling that you'll let anyone down, you'll transform your mind and start fulfilling your leadership potential.

The Drive for More Exercise

Let's put a futuristic spin on this exercise. Compile a list of the people, things, and accomplishments that are most important for you to have in your life. Next, define a time period for when you want to have these things and what they will mean to you. If you're more inclined to look further ahead, set a cap of three to five years. If you prefer to focus on shorter ranges, define a period of six months or one year. There's value in specificity. Get specific, and prioritize what means the most to you.

Champion's Checklist (Tools and Takeaways)

☑ Fulfilling your potential and helping your team members to fulfill their potential is a reciprocal relationship.

☑ Work with your human resources and recruiting department to identify the leadership and personal qualities that you want prospective team members to have.

- ☑ Don't compromise your standard of performance. Set the bar high, work hard to get there, and help others get there, too.
- ☑ Keep in mind the importance of soft skills and emotional intelligence in the hiring process.
- ☑ Don't wait for things to come to you. Take action on what you know is right and in alignment with your game plan.

The Champion's Watch

Forever etched in my memory are the cheers of jubilation echoing throughout the gymnasium.

As I raced up and down the basketball court in seventh grade, there was my dad on the sideline, roaring with approval. Every made shot. Louder. Every rebound. Louder. Every assist. LOUDER. His face beaming with pride and happiness. My heart full of joy.

He was rooting for me then. He rooted for me throughout every endeavor of my life. I truly believe he roots for me now from above, in spirit.

That hour on the basketball hardwood during my middle school days is a small snapshot of the way my dad raised his three boys. My dad was the *ultimate* champion leader for his children.

My dad wasn't just someone who cheered from a distance. He was a hands-on father who directed, corrected, motivated, inspired, coached, and taught us countless life lessons. Throughout my life he wrote me handwritten notes of encouragement and instruction. Whether I was playing a game, broadcasting one, writing an article for my school newspaper, struggling to adjust to a new city or job, or writing a graduate school paper, he was there to support me.

His direct feedback wasn't always filled with praise. He wanted us to know right from wrong. He wanted us to be better than we were the day before. He wanted us to learn and grow. Imbued in his words was a steadfast belief that we could always be better—that we could always feel better.

And, like I understood with the manager of my college radio station—I knew the difference. That difference was just how much he cared for me. How much he loved me. For him, to spend that time helping his sons was what it meant to be a father.

When my dad, William O'Neil Connors, passed in October of 2022, I began to reflect on his life and his incredible legacy. My dad was an empathetic listener who wanted to follow along and be a part of each experience with us. Of course, in the moment, I didn't always realize how much he was helping me process ideas, express emotions, and figure out more of who I was and who I wanted to be.

My dad attended all of our sporting events. It's exactly what I do now for my three sons, coaching many of their teams and cheering on from the sidelines with pride and joy. When you lead with that love, you couldn't possibly see it or have it any other way. You're there. You're in it with maximum focus, attention, and care.

My dad was always there throughout our childhoods and managed to make it to countless life events, even as I moved away from home. When I forgot my shoes on a college basketball road trip, he was there, to comfort me. He was there to take my phone calls as I contemplated some of the biggest decisions of my life.

And on one of the most meaningful days of my life, the day of my wedding, he was there. Seated right behind me in the church. That was no coincidence. My dad always had my back.

The Champion's Watch is a lifetime journey. It's an altruistic and authentic way of living. It desires the best in thought, word, and action for yourself and everyone around you. It starts at the core of who you are as a person and carries outward to every part of your life, especially how you lead. It's an infinite quest of seeking betterment, not at the cost of exhaustion or despair but out of passion and a competitive spirit that seeks contentment.

The beauty is that you have this opportunity every day. It's a long game that's never won in the early stages. It's an accumulation of small wins every day that give you the energy and motivation to press forward with hope, belief, and perseverance.

I hope you will have someone—a champion leader—who believes in you and helps support your dreams and goals as much as my dad believed in and supported me and my brothers.

I hope that you will be that champion leader for others.

Leadership Resources

Self-Awareness Game Plan

Here is the "self-awareness game plan" template that you can use to begin building your own game plan (with a few bonuses). The key is listed, again, at the end.

Passion:

____

____

____

____

____

Values:

____

____

____

____

____

Strengths:

Purpose:

Mission (Definition of Success):

Success Measures:

Goals (SMART):

Bonus:

Current Business and Emotional Intelligence Skills:

Business and Emotional Intelligence Skills You Desire to Have:

____

____

____

____

____

Key

- **Passion:** The things that light the fire inside of you—which drive, motivate, and inspire you every time you think about them or do them.
- **Values:** A set of guiding principles and ideals that provide a standard for the way you behave and make decisions.
- **Strengths:** Your natural talents combined with the skills that you've acquired throughout your career. The things that you naturally do well.
- **Purpose:** Why you're doing what you're doing (the driving force or reasons behind setting your mission and goals).
- **Mission:** How you define success. If you're living and doing this, you will feel fulfilled, happy, and successful. You'll know that your actions have meaning.
- **Success measures:** Standards by which we determine whether our actions are living up to our mission (definition of success).
- **Goals:** Set "SMART" goals (the tangible results you desire to achieve). SMART stands for specific, measurable, achievable, relevant, and time-bound. George T. Doran first coined this term over 40 years ago. It's a clever mnemonic and easy-to-remember acronym that gives us a framework for goal setting.

Leadership Resources

Connecting with Christopher and Additional Learning

- *Visit Christopher's website*: https://chrisdconnors.com.

  On Christopher's website, you will find blog articles, leadership resources, and details of his books: *The Value of You* and *Emotional Intelligence for the Modern Leader.* Subscribe to Christopher's newsletter to get exclusive tips and stories on how to lead like a champion.

- *Executive and Leadership Coaching*

  Christopher provides executive and leadership coaching to individuals and teams. If you're looking to champion your career, become a more emotionally intelligent leader, or help elevate the leadership abilities of your team and organization, please send him a message to connect.

- *Keynote Speaking and Team-Building Workshops*

  Christopher is a globally recognized keynote speaker on the topics of emotional intelligence, championship leadership, and leading through change.

  He also provides energizing and inspiring team-building events and leadership workshops for organizations all around the world. Reach out to him via his website to connect.

- *Consulting*

  Christopher also provides leadership consulting services to top, global organizations on a limited basis. If you're looking to build a championship culture, reach out to him via his website to connect.

- *Check out Christopher's LinkedIn Learning course: Leading with Emotional Intelligence.*

  This is a video-based course that provides you with a leadership foundation in emotional intelligence. Christopher shows you how to lead by using emotional intelligence to your advantage.

- *Connect with Christopher on LinkedIn: Christopher D. Connors (chrisdconnors). Subscribe to Christopher's newsletter on LinkedIn: The Champion Leader Movement.*
- *Follow Christopher on YouTube: @chrisdconnors.*
- *Follow Christopher on X (Twitter): @chris_connors42.*

Notes

People Come First

1. "The Impact of Employee Engagement on Performance," *Harvard Business Review* Analytic Services, https://hbr.org/resources/pdfs/comm/achievers/hbr_achievers_report_sep13.pdf.
2. "Herb Kelleher & Building a People-Focused Culture," HSMAmericas, YouTube video, https://www.youtube.com/watch?v=oxTFA1kh1m8.
3. "Pearson Skills Outlook: Power Skills," Pearson, https://plc.pearson.com/en-GB/insights/pearson-skills-outlook-powerskills.
4. Hess, Abigail Johnson, "'The Great Reimagination of Work': Why 50% of Workers Want to Make a Career Change," Make It, CNBC, October 12, 2021, https://www.cnbc.com/2021/10/12/why-50percent-of-workers-want-to-make-a-career-change-new-survey.html.
5. Kelleher, Herb, "How Southwest Airlines Built Its Culture," WOBI – World of Business Ideas, YouTube, October 20, 2016, https://www.youtube.com/watch?v=8_CeFiUkV7s.

Chapter 1

1. Hirsch, Jeffrey, interview by the author.
2. "The Future Is Flexible," Achievers Workforce Institute 2023 Engagement and Retention Report, n.d., www.achievers.com/wp-content/uploads/2023/01/Achievers-Workforce-Institute_2023-Engagement-and-Retention_Flexible-Future.pdf.
3. "What Is Empathy?" Greater Good Magazine, n.d., https://greatergood.berkeley.edu/topic/empathy/definition.

4. "Indra K. Nooyi on Performance with Purpose," Boston Consulting Group, January 14, 2010, https://www.bcg.com/publications/2010/indra-nooyi-performance-purpose.
5. Dictionary.com. 'Authentic'. Retrieved from https://www.dictionary.com/browse/authentic.
6. "7 Career Lessons from Billionaire Abigail Johnson," Forbes, November 1, 2013, www.forbes.com/sites/moiraforbes/2013/11/01/seven-career-lessons-from-billionaire-abigail-johnson/?sh=72319ee776a1.
7. Harter, Jim, and Amy Adkins, "Employees Want a Lot More from Their Managers," Gallup, n.d., www.gallup.com/workplace/236570/employees-lot-managers.aspx.

Chapter 2

1. Salovey, Peter, and John D. Mayer, "Emotional Intelligence," *Sage Journals* 9, no. 3 (March 1990), https://journals.sagepub.com/doi/10.2190/DUGG-P24E-52WK-6CDG.
2. Connors, Christopher D., *The Value of You: The Guide to Living Boldly and Joyfully through the Power of Core Values*, November 3, 2017, Patricia William Publishing.
3. Walsh, Lisa C., Julia K. Boehm, and Sonja Lyubomirsky, "Does Happiness Promote Career Success" Revisiting the Evidence," *Journal of Career Assessment* 26, no. 2 (January 2018): 199–219, https://sonjalyubomirsky.com/files/2012/09/Walsh-Boehm-Lyubomirsky-2018-1.pdf.
4. Feloni, Richard, "Google's Eric Schmidt Explains the 2 Most Important Traits a Job Candidate Can Have," Business Insider, June 10, 2017, https://www.businessinsider.com/google-eric-schmidt-most-important-traits-job-candidate-2017-6.
5. Eurich, Tasha, "What Self-Awareness Really Is (and How to Cultivate It)," *Harvard Business Review*, January 4, 2018, https://hbr.org/2018/01/what-self-awareness-really-is-and-how-to-cultivate-it.
6. "Women in the Workplace 2022. Part 2: Why Women Leaders Are Switching Jobs," n.d., https://leanin.org/women-in-the-workplace/2022/why-women-leaders-are-switching-jobs.
7. Coburn-Litvak, Pamela, interview by the author.

8. Karunaratne, Yenushka, interview by the author.
9. Chng, Daniel Han Ming, Tae-Yeol Kim, Brad Gilbreath, and Lynne Anderson, "Why People Believe in Their Leaders—on Not," *MIT Sloan Management Review*, August 17, 2018, https://sloanreview.mit.edu/article/why-people-believe-in-their-leaders-or-not/.
10. "Vicarious and Self-Reinforcement Process," Scribd, n.d., https://www.scribd.com/document/443787168/Vicarious-and-self-reinforcement-process-pdf.
11. Bandura, Albert, *Social Foundations of Thought and Action: A Social Cognitive Theory*, 1986, Englewood Cliffs: Prentice Hall.
12. Bandura, Albert, "Self-efficacy: Toward a Unifying Theory of Behavioral Change," *Psychological Review* 84, no 2 (March 1977): 191–215.
13. Bloom, Stacie, "Your Brain on Confidence: Fake it 'til You Make It," *Wall Street Journal* (content by Deloitte), April 8, 2021, https://deloitte.wsj.com/riskandcompliance/your-brain-on-confidence-fake-it-til-you-make-it-01617908527.
14. Sutton, Robert I., "Learning from Success and Failure," *Harvard Business Review*, June 4, 2007, https://hbr.org/2007/06/learning-from-success-and-fail.

Chapter 3

1. "Coach K's Defining Moment," ESPN, n.d., https://www.espn.com/video/clip/_/id/12162127.
2. "An Introduction to the Individualization CliftonStrengths Theme," Gallup, n.d., www.gallup.com/cliftonstrengths/en/252272/individualization-theme.aspx.
3. Stillman, Jessica, "The 3 Essentials Every Great Leader Must Have, According to Microsoft CEO Satya Nadella," *Inc.*, November 12, 2018, www.inc.com/jessica-stillman/the-3-characteristics-all-great-leaders-share-according-to-microsoft-ceo-satya-nadella.html.
4. LoGiurato, Brett, "Neuroscience Can Help You Become a Better Leader," *Knowledge at Wharton Podcast*, October 27, 2020, https://knowledge.wharton.upenn.edu/podcast/knowledge-at-wharton-podcast/neuroscience-can-help-you-become-a-better-leader/.

5. "Why Multitasking Doesn't Work" Cleveland Clinic, March 10, 2021, https://health.clevelandclinic.org/science-clear-multitasking-doesnt-work/.
6. Santi, Jenny, "The Secret to Happiness Is Helping Others," *Time*, August 4, 2017, https://time.com/collection-post/4070299/secret-to-happiness/.
7. Wolpert, Stuart, "UCLA Neuroscientist's Book Explains Why Social Connection Is as Important as Food and Shelter," UCLA Newsroom, October 10, 2013, https://newsroom.ucla.edu/releases/we-are-hard-wired-to-be-social-248746.
8. Gavin, Matt, "How to Become a More Resilient Leader," Harvard Business School Online, Business Insights, December 17, 2019, https://online.hbs.edu/blog/post/resilient-leadership.
9. Whitfield, Karen M., and Kyle John Wilby, "Developing Grit, Motivation, and Resilience: To Give Up on Giving In," National Library of Medicine, June 9, 2021, www.ncbi.nlm.nih.gov/pmc/articles/PMC8293386/.
10. Snyder, Mark, "Tom Brady: Mantra of U-M's Jon Falk Inspires Me," *Detroit Free Press*, September 10, 2015, www.freep.com/story/sports/college/university-michigan/wolverines/2015/09/10/michigan-football-tom-brady/72005672/.

Chapter 4

1. Barra, Mary, "Mary Barra: Five Lessons from the Kitchen Table," Duke Today, May 8, 2022, https://today.duke.edu/2022/05/mary-barra-five-lessons-kitchen-table.
2. LaReau, Jamie L., "GM CEO Mary Barra's Rare, Behind-the-Scenes Interview: Who She Relies On in 'Lonely Job,'" *Detroit Free Press*, June 3, 2022, https://www.freep.com/in-depth/money/cars/general-motors/2022/06/03/gm-ceo-mary-barra-reveals-personal-details-rare-interview/9705679002/.
3. Jiang, Serina, "General Motors CEO Mary Barra Shares Her Leadership Journey, Visions for the Future," *The Michigan Daily*, April 13, 2022, https://www.michigandaily.com/news/general-motors-ceo-mary-barra-shares-her-leadership-journey-visions-for-the-future/.
4. Barra, Mary, "Mary Barra: Five Lessons from the Kitchen Table," Duke Today, May 8, 2022, https://today.duke.edu/2022/05/mary-barra-five-lessons-kitchen-table.

5. Heath, Chip, and Dan Heath, *Made to Stick: Why Some Ideas Survive and Others Die*, 2007, Random House.
6. Koss, Hal, "7 Leadership Lessons from Former Netflix CEO Reed Hastings," Built In, January 20, 2023, https://builtin.com/company-culture/netflix-book.
7. Dweck, Carol, "What Having a 'Growth Mindset' Actually Means," *Harvard Business Review*, January 13, 2016, https://hbr.org/2016/01/what-having-a-growth-mindset-actually-means.
8. Gino, Francesca, "The Business Case for Curiosity," *Harvard Business Review*, September–October 2018, https://hbr.org/2018/09/the-business-case-for-curiosity.
9. Forbes, Moira, "7 Career Lessons from Billionaire Abigail Johnson," *Forbes*, November 1, 2013, https://www.forbes.com/sites/moiraforbes/2013/11/01/seven-career-lessons-from-billionaire-abigail-johnson/?sh=77a8f3c976a1.

Chapter 5

1. Shetty Jay, "Susan Wojcicki & Jay Shetty on Avoiding Burnout as a Leader," Jay Shetty Blog, March 28, 2023, https://jayshetty.me/blog/susan-wojcicki-and-jay-shetty-on-avoiding-burnout-as-a-leader/.
2. Feinberg, Paul, "Former YouTube CEO Says Successful Companies Double Down on Core Competencies," UCLA Anderson School of Management, March 29, 2023, https://www.anderson.ucla.edu/news-and-events/former-youtube-ceo-says-successful-companies-double-down-core-competencies.
3. Graham, Paul, "Maker's Schedule, Manager's Schedule," Paul Graham website, July 2009, www.paulgraham.com/makersschedule.html.
4. Project Management Institute (PMI). (2022). Process Groups: A Practice Guide. PMI.
5. Sima, Richard, "Trouble Achieving Goals? Why Your Brain Needs Reminders," *Washington Post*, July 27, 2023, www.washingtonpost.com/wellness/2023/07/27/reminders-goals-cognitive-offloading-strategies/?=undefined.
6. Csikszentmihalyi, Mihaly, *Flow: The Psychology of Optimal Experience*, 2008, Harper Perennial Modern Classics.

7. Fogg, BJ, *Tiny Habits: The Small Changes That Change Everything*, 2020, Harvest.
8. Miller, Tessa, "We Are Katia Beauchamp and Hayley Barna, Founders of Birchbox, and This Is How We Work," Life Hacker, March 27, 2013, https://lifehacker.com/we-are-katia-beauchamp-and-hayley-barna-founders-of-bi-5992574.

Chapter 6

1. Weitz, Richard, interview by the author.
2. Barhite, Britany, "Executive Communication: Is the Door Really Open?" Firstup Blog, August 4, 2022, https://firstup.io/blog/executive-communication-is-the-door-really-open/.
3. Hannon, Patricia, "Are You Listening?" *Stanford Medicine Magazine*, May 21, 2018, https://stanmed.stanford.edu/modern-medicine-challenges-the-bonds-between-doctors-and-patients/.
4. "The Cost of Poor Communications," SHRM, n.d., www.shrm.org/resourcesandtools/hr-topics/behavioral-competencies/communication/pages/the-cost-of-poor-communications.aspx.
5. Cuddy, Amy J.C., Caroline A. Wilmuth, Andy J. Yap, Dana R. Carney, "Preparatory Power Posing Affects Nonverbal Presence and Job Interview Performance," Haas School of Business, University of California Berkeley, n.d., https://faculty.haas.berkeley.edu/dana_carney/pp_performance.pdf.
6. Knowledge at Wharton Staff, "Better Communication through Neuroscience," Knowledge at Wharton, October 13, 2020, https://knowledge.wharton.upenn.edu/article/better-communication-neuroscience/.
7. Barker, Eric, "The Simple Thing That Makes the Happiest People in the World So Happy," *Time*, April 13, 2014, https://time.com/59684/the-simple-thing-that-makes-the-happiest-people-in-the-world-so-happy/.
8. Lyubomirsky, Sonja, *The How of Happiness: A New Approach to Getting the Life You Want*, December 30, 2008, Penguin Books.
9. Jassy, Andy, "Update from Andy Jassy on Return to Office Plans," Amazon Company News, February 17, 2023, www.aboutamazon.com/news/company-news/andy-jassy-update-on-amazon-return-to-office.

10. Yang, Longgi, Sonia Jaffe, Siddharth Suri, Shilpi Sinha, Jeffrey Weston, Connor Joyce, Neha Parikh Shah, Kevin Sherman, Brent Hecht, and Jaime Teevan, "The Effects of Remote Work on Collaboration among Information Workers," *Nature Human Behavior*, September 2021, www.microsoft.com/en-us/research/publication/the-effects-of-remote-work-on-collaboration-among-information-workers/.
11. Sherman, Alex, and Sarah Whitten, "Bob Iger Tells Disney Employees They Must Return to the Office Four Days a Week," CNBC, January 9, 2023, www.cnbc.com/2023/01/09/disney-ceo-bob-iger-tells-employees-to-return-to-the-office-four-days-a-week.html.
12. Duhigg, Charles, "What Google Learned from Its Quest to Build the Perfect Team," *The New York Times Magazine* 26, 2016, www.nytimes.com/2016/02/28/magazine/what-google-learned-from-its-quest-to-build-the-perfect-team.html.
13 . Edmondson, Amy C., "Psychological Safety," Amy C. Edmondson's website, https://amycedmondson.com/psychological-safety/.

Chapter 7

1. "How Southwest Airlines Built Its Culture | Herb Kelleher | WOBI," WOBI – World of Business Ideas, YouTube, October 20, 2016, https://www.youtube.com/watch?v=8_CeFiUkV7s.
2. Erwin, Mike, "In a Distracted World, Solitude Is a Competitive Advantage," *Harvard Business Review*, October 19, 2017, https://hbr.org/2017/10/in-a-distracted-world-solitude-is-a-competitive-advantage.
3. "Steve Jobs' 2005 Stanford Commencement Address," Stanford, June 12, 2005, YouTube, https://www.youtube.com/watch?v=UF8uR6Z6KLc.
4. Ibid.

Chapter 8

1. Hirsch, Jeffrey, interview by the author.
2. "The Future of Streaming and Diverse Content: Starz CEO Jeffrey Hirsch Weighs In," McKinsey & Company, Interview, March 4, 2022, www

.mckinsey.com/industries/technology-media-and-telecommunications/our-insights/the-future-of-streaming-and-diverse-content-starz-ceo-jeffrey-hirsch-weighs-in.

3. "7 C's of Leadership: Working with Others," MasterClass, n.d., www.masterclass.com/classes/indra-nooyi-teaches-leading-with-purpose/chapters/7-c-s-of-leadership-working-with-others.
4. Kahneman, Daniel, *Thinking, Fast and Slow*, April 2, 2013, Farrar, Straus and Giroux.
5. Duarte, Nancy, *Resonate: Present Visual Stories That Transform Audiences*, September 28, 2010, John Wiley and Sons.
6. "A Tactical Guide to Managing Up: 30 Tips from the Smartest People We Know," First Round, n.d., https://review.firstround.com/a-tactical-guide-to-managing-up-30-tips-from-the-smartest-people-we-know.
7. Ibid.
8. Strock, James M. "Theodore Roosevelt's 20 Key Elements of Leadership," n.d., https://www.pnbhs.school.nz/wp-content/uploads/2015/11/Teddy-Roosevelt-20-Key-Elements-of-Leadership.pdf.
9. Dahl, John, *Rounders*, Miramax Films, 1998, 121 minutes, https://www.miramax.com/movie/Rounders/.
10. Cain, Susan, "The Rise of the New Groupthink," *New York Times*, January 13, 2012, www.nytimes.com/2012/01/15/opinion/sunday/the-rise-of-the-new-groupthink.html.
11. Cialdini, Robert, *Pre-Suasion: A Revolutionary Way to Influence and Persuade*, June 5, 2018, Simon & Schuster. https://www.amazon.com/Pre-Suasion-Revolutionary-Way-Influence-Persuade/dp/1501109804.
12. Nooyi, Indra, "Connect with Your Team," MasterClass, n.d., www.masterclass.com/classes/indra-nooyi-teaches-leading-with-purpose/chapters/connect-with-your-team.
13. Cuddy, Amy J.C., Matthew Kohut, and John Neffinger, "Connect, Then Lead," *Harvard Business Review*, July–August 2013, https://hbr.org/2013/07/connect-then-lead.
14. Hess, James D., "Enhancing Decisions and Decision-Making Processes through the Application of Emotional Intelligence Skills," *Management Decision* 49, no. 5: 710–721, https://doi.org/10.1108/00251741111130805.

15. "What Is Strategic Intuition," Columbia Press, n.d., https://columbiapress.typepad.com/strategic_intuition/what-is-stra.html.

Chapter 9

1. Duffy, Clare, "From the Brink of Bankruptcy to a 1,300% Stock Gain: How This CEO Turned around Her Company," *CNN Business*, March 27, 2020, https://edition.cnn.com/2020/03/27/tech/lisa-su-amd-risk-takers/index.html.
2. Ibid.
3. Bryant, Adam, "Lisa Su on the Art of Setting Ambitious Goals," *New York Times*, May 19, 2017, https://www.nytimes.com/2017/05/19/business/lisa-su-on-the-art-of-setting-ambitious-goals.html.
4. Ibid.
5. "Fanatics to Make Medical Gear Instead of Baseball Uniforms," ESPN, March 26, 2020, www.espn.com/mlb/story/_/id/28959410/fanatics-make-medical-gear-baseball-uniforms.
6. Burns, Matt, "Tesla Shows How It's Building Ventilators with Car Parts," TechCrunch, April 5, 2020, https://techcrunch.com/2020/04/05/tesla-shows-how-its-building-ventilators-with-car-parts/.
7. LaReau, Jamie L. "GM CEO Mary Barra's Rare, behind-the-Scenes Interview: Who She Relies On In 'Lonely Job,'" *Detroit Free Press*, June 3, 2022, See www.freep.com/in-depth/money/cars/general-motors/2022/06/03/gm-ceo-mary-barra-reveals-personal-details-rare-interview/9705679002/.
8. Vaynerchuk, Gary, "My Personal Definition of Humility: Road to Twelve and a Half (Series), Gary Vaynerchuk website, November 29, 2021, https://garyvaynerchuk.com/my-personal-definition-of-humility-road-to-twelve-and-a-half-series/.
9. Erwin, Mike, "In a Distracted World, Solitude Is a Competitive Advantage," *Harvard Business Review*, October 19, 2017, https://hbr.org/2017/10/in-a-distracted-world-solitude-is-a-competitive-advantage.
10. Willink, Jocko, and Leif Babin, *Extreme Ownership: How U.S. Navy SEALs Lead and Win*, October 20, 2015, St. Martin's Press.

Chapter 10

1. Bloom, Stacie, interview by the author.
2. Kelly, Chiho, interview by the author.
3. Johnson, Michael G., interview by the author.
4. Gien, Brad, interview by the author.
5. "Wooden's Wisdom: How Did You Teach Your Players the Fundamentals?" John Wooden's Wisdom, YouTube, October 11, 2018, https://www.youtube.com/watch?v=1-mSQxH2mvc.
6. "Overconfidence Linked to One's View of Intelligence," Science Daily, March 7,2016,www.sciencedaily.com/releases/2016/03/160307092325.htm.

Chapter 11

1. Jackson, Phil, and Hugh Delehanty, *Eleven Rings: The Soul of Success*, April 29, 2014, Penguin Books
2. "Spiritual Wellness," Wellness at Northwestern, n.d., www.northwestern.edu/wellness/8-dimensions/spiritual-wellness.html.
3. "What We Do," Mercy Corps, n.d., www.mercycorps.org/what-we-do.
4. Jerving, Sara, "Mercy Corps; Tjada Doyen McKenna on Paving the Road for Others," Devex, October 10, 2022, www.devex.com/news/mercy-corps-tjada-d-oyen-mckenna-on-paving-the-road-for-others-104148.
5. "'Give Away Your Legos' and Other Commandments for Scaling Startups," First Round Review, n.d., https://review.firstround.com/give-away-your-legos-and-other-commandments-for-scaling-startups.
6. Pantra, Kevin, "Chiefs' Patrick Mahomes: I Would've Had to Learn to Play QB 'Different Way' than I Want without Andy Reid," NFL, July 13, 2023,https://www.nfl.com/news/chiefs-patrick-mahomes-i-would-ve-had-to-learn-to-play-qb-different-way-than-i-w.
7. Bilas, Jay, *Toughness: Developing True Strength On and Off the Court*, March 4, 2014, Berkeley. https://www.amazon.com/Toughness-Developing-True-Strength-Court/dp/0451414683.
8. Knight, Phil, *Shoe Dog: A Memoir by the Creator of Nike*, April 26, 2016, Scribner. https://www.amazon.com/Shoe-Dog-Memoir-Creator-Nike/dp/1501135910.

9. Achor, Shawn, *The Happiness Advantage: The Seven Principles of Positive Psychology That Fuel Success and Performance at Work*, September 14, 2010, Crown Currency. https://www.amazon.com/Happiness-Advantage-Principles-Psychology-Performance/dp/0307591549.
10. Kipling, Rudyard, *The Jungle Book*, 1894, Macmillan. https://www.amazon.com/Jungle-Book-Rudyard-Kipling/dp/1503332543.

Chapter 12

1. Thomas, Jack, "Hitting 101 by Tony Gwynn December 2009," Jack Thomas, YouTube, December 30, 2009, https://www.youtube.com/watch?v=GhVSBMjLwsA.
2. Tomova, Livia, Kimberly L. Wang, Todd Thompson, Gillian A. Matthews, Atsushi Takahashi, Kay M. Tye, and Rebecca Saxe, "Acute Social Isolation Evokes Midbrain Craving Responses Similar to Hunger," *Nature Neuroscience* 23, no. 12 (2020): 1597–1605, https://www.nature.com/articles/s41593-020-00742-z, updated version: https://www.nature.com/articles/s41593-021-01004-2.
3. Trafton, Anne, "A Hunger for Social Contact," MIT News, November 23, 2020, https://news.mit.edu/2020/hunger-social-cravings-neuroscience-1123.
4. Hopper, Elizabeth, "Can Helping Others Help You Find Meaning in Life?" *Greater Good Magazine*, February 16, 2016, https://greatergood.berkeley.edu/article/item/can_helping_others_help_you_find_meaning_in_life.
5. Van Tongeren, Daryl R., Jeffrey D. Green, Don E. Davis, Joshua N. Hook, and Timothy L. Hulsey, "Prosociality Enhances Meaning in Life," *The Journal of Positive Psychology* 11, no. 3, 225–236, https://doi.org/10.1080/17439760.2015.1048814.
6. "Seventy-One Percent of Employers Say They Value Emotional Intelligence over IQ, According to CareerBuilder Survey" CareerBuilder, August 18, 2011, https://press.careerbuilder.com/2011-08-18-Seventy-One-Percent-of-Employers-Say-They-Value-Emotional-Intelligence-Over-IQ-According-to-CareerBuilder-Survey.
7. "The Hard Truth about Soft Skills," AMA, American Management Association, January 24, 2019, www.amanet.org/articles/the-hard-truth-about-soft-skills/.

8. Zenger, Jack, and Joseph Folkman, "How Managers Drive Results and Employee Engagement at the Same Time," *Harvard Business Review*, June 19, 2017, https://hbr.org/2017/06/how-managers-drive-results-and-employee-engagement-at-the-same-time.
9. Sherman, Jeremy E., "Faith: What Is It and Who Has It?" *Psychology Today*, September 12, 2013, https://www.psychologytoday.com/us/blog/ambigamy/201309/faith-what-is-it-and-who-has-it.

The Champion Leader—Acknowledgments

First, I want to thank God for His incredible grace and love. I truly believe my steps have been guided by Him. I'm thankful for the many blessings He has provided to me, and I'm appreciative of the opportunity to share my voice with the world.

Thank you to the team at Wiley for bringing this book to life. Thank you to my editors, Georgette Beatty and Zachary Schisgal, for your guidance and for helping me turn my ideas into a book I am very proud of.

To my wife, Tosha: my rock and life partner. Thank you for showing me and our family what championship leadership is all about. We love you and thank you for all of the incredible sacrifices you make for our family!

To my beautiful boys, Roman, Dominic, and Ciarán: I cannot express in words just how much I love and care for you. I wish you a lifetime of happiness, love, and growth. I will always be there for you and do the best I can to be the champion leader you deserve.

To my mom: I admire your grace, kindness, thoughtfulness, and tremendous love for me and your family. You are the best mom I could ever ask for. Like Dad, you are a champion leader who helped provide me with a foundation to create the life of my dreams. Thank you!

To my brothers, Kevin and Bill: Where would I be without your brotherly friendship, support, and love? OK, let's not answer that one!

Kevin: I truly believe you're the best sportscaster on television. You're an even better brother, husband, and father. Thank you for always being there for me and for showing me so many lessons in championship leadership throughout the years.

Bill: Like Kevin, you're an amazing father, husband, and brother. I admire your perseverance, kindness, and generosity. You've set an awesome example of leadership for your children, and you will continue to be an awesome asset to every organization you work with.

To my mother-in-law, Jackie Allawos: Thank you for your dedication to our family. Your love for all of us, especially our three boys, is unrivaled. We are extremely grateful to have you in our lives.

Thank you to Richard Weitz for being a great client and friend. I know you will continue to positively influence everyone you meet.

Thank you to Jeffrey Hirsch for your incredible leadership wisdom and for modeling what championship leadership is all about.

Special thanks to Yenushka Karunaratne and Pamela Coburn-Litvak for sharing your amazing knowledge and guidance.

To the interviewees for Chapter 10: Chiho Kelly, Brad Gien, Stacie Bloom, and Michael Johnson—thank you for your time and for sharing your own brand of championship leadership!

Thank you to Ryan Bamford. I admire the way you lead your organization and how you lead your family. You're a great man and true friend.

Special thanks to Steve and Kathy Hill, Brian Reilly, Nils Bosch, Brian Punger, Ron Carman, Rob Stewart, Kelly Ellis, Mariam Hutchinson, Tanya Boyd, José Dominguez, Sam Shriver, MJ Hall, Michael Thompson, David Esoldo, Andrea Hinkle, Bobby Pollicino, Patrick Mulloy, and Jasmine Bell.

To my grandmother, Mary Reilly, Fr. Owen Shelley, and Owen Reilly: you are thought of often, and I'll cherish my memories of you forever.

Thank you to the many clients I've worked with and partnered with over the years. I'm grateful for every opportunity to share the message of championship leadership and emotional intelligence with new organizations.

Thank you to everyone who has ever believed in me and given me an opportunity to succeed. I will always be there for you.

To my dad, this book is dedicated to your remarkable life. I think of you every day. I love you.

And last but certainly not least, thank you to you, the reader. It's an honor to share these words with you in the hope that you will live and lead at your best.

I genuinely believe the best is yet to come.

Biography (About the Author)

Christopher D. Connors is a #1 best-selling author, keynote speaker, executive coach, and globally recognized expert on emotional intelligence. He helps leaders increase their emotional intelligence, achieve results, and build thriving organizations. Christopher consults with executives and leaders at Fortune 1000 companies and with organizations spanning many industries. His writing has appeared in World Economic Forum, CNBC, Thrive Global, and Medium. His book *Emotional Intelligence for the Modern Leader* is one of the top selling emotional intelligence books in the world.

Christopher's first book, *The Value of You*, has helped thousands of professionals create an authentic, values-based life. His video-based course, *Leading with Emotional Intelligence*, is a top leadership course on LinkedIn Learning.

Christopher's business and coaching experience comes from working with CEOs, top leaders, and organizations from around the world. He is one of the most in-demand leadership speakers in the world. He's worked with William Morris Endeavor (WME), Northrop Grumman, US Army, Edward Jones, Merrill Lynch, GitLab, the Florida State Government, McKesson, Google, and many more similar organizations.

Christopher is happily married to his lovely southern belle CEO wife and is the proud father of three large, rambunctious sports-loving boys. He lives in Mount Pleasant, South Carolina. Visit him at: https://chrisdconnors.com/.

Index

Page numbers followed by *f* refer to figures.